ORIGO
STEPPING STONES

COMPREHENSIVE MATHEMATICS

AUTHORS

James Burnett
Calvin Irons
Peter Stowasser
Allan Turton

PROGRAM CONSULTANTS

Diana Lambdin
Frank Lester, Jr.
Kit Norris

CONTRIBUTING WRITERS

Debi DePaul
Beth Lewis

STUDENT BOOK B

ORIGO
EDUCATION

CONTENTS

ORIGO Stepping Stones • Grade 4

CONTENTS

Step In

Two friends share the cost of the remote control car.

$68

$74

What amount should they each pay?
How do you know?

Imagine they share the cost of the helicopter.
How could you calculate the amount they each pay?

Layla uses blocks.

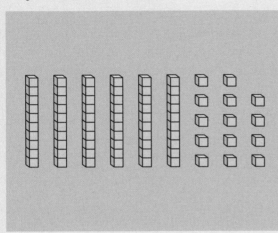

Cody uses multiplication.

$2 \times \boxed{} = 74$

$2 \times 35 = 70$ $35 each is not enough.
$2 \times 40 = 80$ $40 each is too much.
$2 \times 36 = 72$ $36 each is almost enough.

so

$2 \times 37 = 74$ They each pay $37.

Look carefully at Layla's blocks.
Why did she regroup 7 tens and 4 ones for 6 tens and 14 ones?

Look carefully at Cody's strategy.
How did he calculate the amount each person should pay?

Step Up

I. Complete each of these. Use blocks to help your thinking.

a.

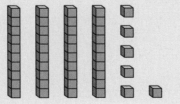

Half of 46 is $\boxed{}$

$46 \div 2 = \boxed{}$

b.

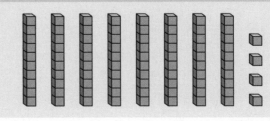

Half of 84 is $\boxed{}$

$84 \div 2 = \boxed{}$

© ORIGO Education

2. Complete each equation. Show your thinking.

a.

$62 \div 2 =$ ____

b.

$36 \div 2 =$ ____

c.

$70 \div 2 =$ ____

d.

$94 \div 2 =$ ____

3. Halve each number. Show your thinking on page 280.

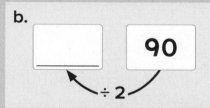

a.

____ 86 ÷ 2

b.

____ 90 ÷ 2

c.

____ 58 ÷ 2

Step Ahead   Solve each problem. Show your thinking.

a. A group of 75 students are asked to line up in pairs. How many students are without a partner?

____

b. Two friends share the cost of a meal. The meal costs $47. What amount should they each pay?

$____ and ____¢

Step In   Look at the numbers on this strip.

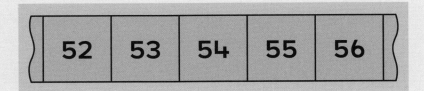

Which numbers could you divide evenly by 2?
What digits did you look at to help you decide?

Which numbers could you divide by 4?

Write numbers in this diagram to show your thinking.

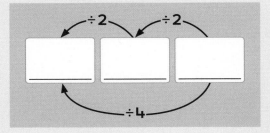

Think double double to multiply by 4.
Think halve halve to divide by 4.

How could you extend this strategy to divide by 8?

What number on the strip can you divide by 8?

Step Up   1. Write the missing numbers. Then complete each equation.

a.
72 ÷ 4 = ☐

Half of 72 = 36

Half of 36 = ____

b.
96 ÷ 8 = ☐

Half of ____ = ____

Half of ____ = ____

Half of ____ = ____

c.
92 ÷ 4 = ☐

Half of ____ = ____

Half of ____ = ____

2. Complete each diagram. Show your thinking on page 280.

a.
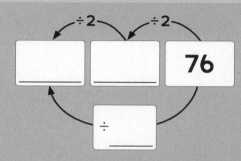
÷2 ÷2 ÷2

[ ] [ ] [ ] 160

÷ [ ]

b.
÷2 ÷2

[ ] [ ] 100

÷ [ ]

c.
÷2 ÷2

[ ] [ ] 76

÷ [ ]

d.
÷2 ÷2 ÷2

[ ] [ ] [ ] 104

÷ [ ]

3. Complete each equation. Show your thinking.

a.
96 ÷ 4 = [ ]

b.
120 ÷ 8 = [ ]

c.
108 ÷ 4 = [ ]

Step Ahead Use the halving strategy to solve this problem.

○ $360

Eight friends share the cost of this gift. What amount should they each pay?

$_____ each

Computation Practice   Why is B the hottest letter in the alphabet?

★ Complete the equations. Then write each letter above its matching answer at the bottom of the page.

$180 + 350 =$ ____ **a**	$620 - 380 =$ ____ **e**	$560 - 280 =$ ____ **i**
$250 + 490 =$ ____ **i**	$470 + 460 =$ ____ **l**	$610 - 450 =$ ____ **b**
$640 - 380 =$ ____ **b**	$270 + 390 =$ ____ **e**	$420 + 290 =$ ____ **o**
$820 - 530 =$ ____ **a**	$360 - 180 =$ ____ **u**	$560 + 250 =$ ____ **t**
$490 + 380 =$ ____ **m**	$940 - 370 =$ ____ **l**	$730 - 560 =$ ____ **i**
$570 + 340 =$ ____ **s**	$380 + 560 =$ ____ **c**	$830 - 470 =$ ____ **e**
$940 - 180 =$ ____ **s**	$170 + 260 =$ ____ **o**	$370 + 270 =$ ____ **k**

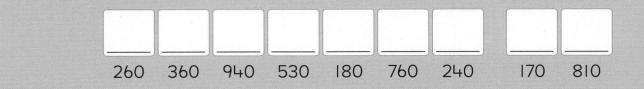

260 360 940 530 180 760 240   170 810

870 290 640 660 910   430 280 570   160 710 740 930

Ongoing Practice

I. Use a protractor to help you find these angles.

- Write **A** next to the acute angles.
- Write **R** next to the right angles.
- Write **O** next to the obtuse angles.

a.

b.

FROM 4.6.11

2. Complete each equation. Show your thinking.

a.

$58 \div 2 = \underline{}$

b.

$74 \div 2 = \underline{}$

FROM 4.7.1

Preparing for Module 8

Write the fact family for each array.

a.

$\underline{} \times \underline{} = \underline{}$

$\underline{} \times \underline{} = \underline{}$

$\underline{} \div \underline{} = \underline{}$

$\underline{} \div \underline{} = \underline{}$

b.

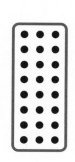

$\underline{} \times \underline{} = \underline{}$

$\underline{} \times \underline{} = \underline{}$

$\underline{} \div \underline{} = \underline{}$

$\underline{} \div \underline{} = \underline{}$

Step In

Look at these jars of marbles.

Imagine you want to share the jar of 34 marbles equally among 4 friends.

How many marbles will be in each share?

How many marbles will be left over?

What thinking did you use to calculate the number of marbles in each share?

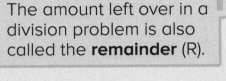

The amount left over in a division problem is also called the **remainder** (R).

I shared 34 cubes into 4 equal groups. There are 2 left over.

I thought of a fours fact that has a product near 34. 8 × 4 = 32. I then have 2 more.

Nancy shares the jar of 22 marbles into bags of 6. How many bags does she use?

How many marbles are left over? How do you know?

Step Up

1. Share each jar of marbles into bags of 5. Write the multiplication fact that helped you calculate the number of bags. Then write the number of marbles left over.

a.

27

☐ × ☐ = ☐

☐ bags with ☐ marbles left over

b.

34

☐ × ☐ = ☐

☐ bags with ☐ marbles left over

2. Share these marbles. Write the multiplication fact that helped you calculate the number in each share. Then write the number left over.

a. 62 marbles shared by 8 people

_____ × _____ = _____

[ ] each, remainder [ ]

b. 50 marbles shared by 7 people

_____ × _____ = _____

[ ] each, remainder [ ]

c. 37 marbles shared by 5 people

_____ × _____ = _____

[ ] each, remainder [ ]

d. 75 marbles shared by 9 people

_____ × _____ = _____

[ ] each, remainder [ ]

3. Think of a multiplication fact to help you solve each division problem. Then write the answer.

a. $17 ÷ 5 =$ [_____] remainder [_____]

b. $32 ÷ 7 =$ [_____] remainder [_____]

c. $22 ÷ 3 =$ [_____] remainder [_____]

d. $39 ÷ 4 =$ [_____] remainder [_____]

e. $49 ÷ 6 =$ [_____] remainder [_____]

f. $51 ÷ 9 =$ [_____] remainder [_____]

Step Ahead

Charlie shares his collection of marbles equally among 5 friends. He then keeps the four marbles left over. Figure out how many marbles might have been in Charlie's collection.

[_____] marbles

Step In — Read each of these problems.

A piece of ribbon is 50 inches long. The ribbon is cut into 6 equal lengths. How long is each piece of ribbon?

6 eggs are packed into each carton. There are 50 eggs. How many egg cartons are filled?

50 students are on a camping trip. 6 students sleep in each tent. How many tents are needed?

What is the same about each problem? What is different?

The remainders mean different things in each problem. How do the remainders help you answer each problem?

The remainder in the first problem could be broken into a fractional amount and shared. Each piece of ribbon is $8\frac{1}{3}$ inches long.

The remainder is not required to answer the second problem. The leftover eggs will not fill a carton.

The remainder in the third problem represents a number of students. These students cannot sleep outside, so another tent is needed.

Step Up

1. Solve each problem. Show your thinking.

a. Teresa is walking 60 miles for charity. She walks 7 miles a day. How many days will it take to complete the walk?

_____ days

b. 20 balls are packed into cans. There are 3 balls in each can. How many balls are left out?

_____ balls

2. Solve each problem. Show your thinking.

a. Riku saves $8 each week to buy a new scooter that costs $74. How many weeks will it be before she can buy the scooter?

◻◻◻ weeks

b. A roll of plastic wrap is 70 meters long. Thomas cuts the plastic wrap into lengths of 9 meters. How many of these lengths can he cut?

◻◻◻ lengths

c. 37 roses have been picked. The roses are sold in bunches of 5. How many bunches can be made?

◻◻◻ bunches

d. A roller coaster has 6 cars. Each seats 8 people. 50 people are waiting. How many will have to wait for the next roller coaster?

◻◻◻ people

Step Ahead

Read the problem. Then write the amount that each person should pay.

$50

Four friends share the cost of this gift. What amount should they each pay?

$ _____ and _____ ¢

Think and Solve

Use the clues to figure out each mystery shape.

Shape 1 Clues

- It is in a row of all polygons.
- It is in a column of all polygons.
- It has a least one right angle.

Shape 2 Clues

- It is in a column that has a circle.
- It is in a row of all polygons.
- It has three acute angles.

Words at Work

Research and write a rule you can use to complete each of these. Then for each number, write one dividend that will divide exactly and one dividend that will not divide exactly. Use dividends greater than 50.

A number can be divided by 2 if

Can be evenly divided by 2 _____   Cannot be evenly divided by 2 _____

A number can be evenly divided by 5 if

Can be evenly divided by 5 _____   Cannot be evenly divided by 5 _____

A number can be evenly divided by 9 if

Can be evenly divided by 9 _____   Cannot be evenly divided by 9 _____

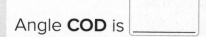

Ongoing Practice

I. Use the clues to calculate the size of each angle in the diagram. Do not use a protector. Show your thinking.

Clues

- Angle **AOE** is 90°.
- Angle **AOB** is 30°.
- Angle **COD** is half of Angle **COE**.
- Angle **COE** is equivalent to Angle **AOB**.

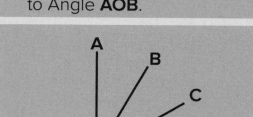

Angle **BOE** is [____]   Angle **COD** is [____]

Angle **BOC** is [____]   Angle **DOE** is [____]

2. Complete each equation. Show your thinking.

a.   76 ÷ 4 = [____]

b.   96 ÷ 8 = [____]

c.   112 ÷ 8 = [____]

Preparing for Module 8

Color the tens part red, and the ones part blue. Then write each product. Add the two partial products and write the total.

6 × 32

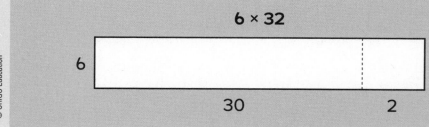

6 × [____] = [____]

6 × [____] = [____]

Total [____]

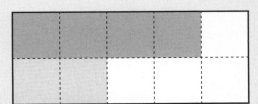

Step In   Leila shaded $\frac{4}{10}$ of this rectangle purple.

She then shaded $\frac{2}{10}$ yellow.

What fraction of the shape did she shade in total?

Complete this equation to match.

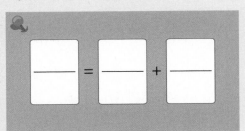

Can you think of another way to shade $\frac{6}{10}$ of the total shape with two colors?

How could you use this number line to calculate $\frac{8}{10} + \frac{3}{10}$?

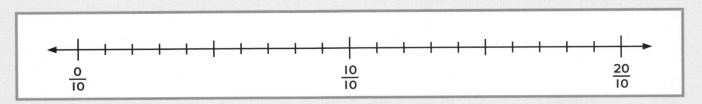

$$\frac{0}{10} \qquad\qquad \frac{10}{10} \qquad\qquad \frac{20}{10}$$

Complete this equation to match.

□/□ + □/□ = □/□

Look at the equation you wrote.

When you add fractions, what happens to the numerator?

What happens to the denominator?

Step Up   1. Each large rectangle is one whole. Shade parts using different colors to show each fraction. Then write the total fraction that is shaded.

a.

$\frac{3}{8} + \frac{4}{8} = \dfrac{}{}$

b.

$\frac{1}{6} + \frac{3}{6} = \dfrac{}{}$

c.

$\frac{4}{10} + \frac{2}{10} = \dfrac{}{}$

2. Use this number line to help you write the totals below.

$$\frac{0}{10} \qquad \frac{10}{10} \qquad \frac{20}{10} \qquad \frac{30}{10}$$

a. $\frac{4}{10} + \frac{5}{10} = $ _____

b. $\frac{6}{10} + \frac{2}{10} = $ _____

c. $\frac{1}{10} + \frac{5}{10} = $ _____

d. $\frac{12}{10} + \frac{7}{10} = $ _____

e. $\frac{5}{10} + \frac{18}{10} = $ _____

f. $\frac{14}{10} + \frac{13}{10} = $ _____

3. Use what you know about adding fractions to complete each equation.

a. $\frac{2}{8} + \frac{5}{8} = $ _____

b. $\frac{7}{6} + \frac{3}{6} = $ _____

c. $\frac{10}{4} + \frac{8}{4} = $ _____

d. $\frac{15}{4} + \frac{3}{4} = $ _____

e. $\frac{5}{3} + \frac{9}{3} + \frac{6}{3} = $ _____

f. $\frac{2}{8} + \frac{15}{8} + \frac{5}{8} = $ _____

g. $\frac{5}{12} + $ _____ $= \frac{9}{12}$

h. _____ $+$ _____ $= \frac{15}{10}$

i. $\frac{11}{12} = $ _____ $+$ _____

j. _____ $+ \frac{7}{10} = \frac{19}{10}$

k. $\frac{23}{10} = $ _____ $+ \frac{18}{10}$

l. _____ $+$ _____ $= \frac{27}{10}$

4. Look at the totals in Question 3. Circle the totals that are greater than 3.

Step Ahead

Write a rule that you could use to add two common fractions with the **same denominator**.

_____

_____

_____

Step In

How could you calculate the total amount of water in these pitchers?

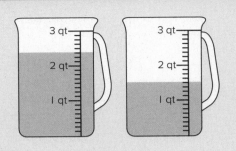

Mia thinks $2\frac{3}{8}$ is equivalent to $2 + \frac{3}{8}$, and $1\frac{4}{8}$ is equivalent to $1 + \frac{4}{8}$.

She wrote this equation.

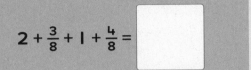

$$2 + \frac{3}{8} + 1 + \frac{4}{8} = \boxed{}$$

She added the whole numbers first.

Next she added the fractions.

Then she added the two totals. What is the total?

Alejandro started with $2\frac{3}{8}$, added 1, then added $\frac{4}{8}$.

Show his method on this number line.

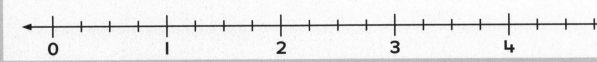

Step Up

1. Use Alejandro's method to add these mixed numbers. Show your thinking on the number line.

a.

$2\frac{2}{4} + 1\frac{1}{4} = \boxed{}$

b.

$2\frac{1}{5} + 1\frac{3}{5} = \boxed{}$

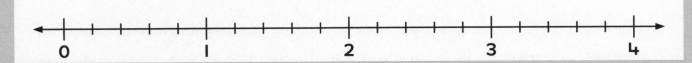

2. Use the same method to add these. Show your thinking on the number line.

a.

$1\frac{3}{10} + \frac{5}{10} = \boxed{}$

b.

$1\frac{4}{8} + 1\frac{3}{8} = \boxed{}$

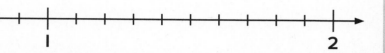

3. Use Mia's method to complete each equation. Show your thinking.

a.

$3\frac{4}{8} + 2\frac{3}{8} = \boxed{}$

b.

$4\frac{3}{6} + 2\frac{2}{6} = \boxed{}$

c.

$3\frac{4}{12} + 5\frac{5}{12} = \boxed{}$

d.

$2\frac{6}{10} + \boxed{} = 7\frac{8}{10}$

e.

$\boxed{} + 1\frac{3}{12} = 5\frac{10}{12}$

f.

$\boxed{} + \boxed{} = 13\frac{6}{8}$

Step Ahead Write the missing numbers on this addition trail.

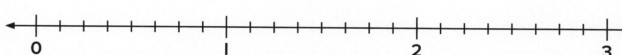

$3\frac{1}{12}$ → +$2\frac{3}{12}$ → $\boxed{}$ → +$5\frac{1}{12}$ → $\boxed{}$ → +$3\frac{4}{12}$ → $\boxed{}$ → +$8\frac{2}{12}$ → $\boxed{}$

Computation Practice

★ Complete the facts as fast as you can. Use the classroom clock to time yourself.

$12 \div 4 = $

$56 \div 8 = $

$16 \div 8 = $

$27 \div 3 = $

$63 \div 9 = $

$30 \div 6 = $

$49 \div 7 = $

$24 \div 8 = $

$45 \div 5 = $

$18 \div 2 = $

$8 \div 1 = $

$64 \div 8 = $

$81 \div 9 = $

$36 \div 4 = $

$42 \div 7 = $

$12 \div 6 = $

$15 \div 3 = $

$72 \div 8 = $

$54 \div 9 = $

$21 \div 3 = $

finish

Ongoing Practice

1. Estimate each total. Then use the standard addition algorithm to calculate the exact total.

a. Estimate

```
    1  8  4  9
+   1  1  0  9
```

b. Estimate

```
    3  5  8  1
+   2  3  7  6
```

c. Estimate

```
    2  9  2  4
+   2  6  0  7
```

2. Share these marbles. Write the multiplication fact that helped you figure out the number in each share. Then write the number left over.

a. 35 marbles shared by 4 people

____ × ____ = ____

[ ] each, remainder [ ]

b. 26 marbles shared by 7 people

____ × ____ = ____

[ ] each, remainder [ ]

c. 48 marbles shared by 5 people

____ × ____ = ____

[ ] each, remainder [ ]

d. 46 marbles shared by 6 people

____ × ____ = ____

[ ] each, remainder [ ]

Preparing for Module 8

Split each number into hundreds, tens, and ones. Think carefully before you write.

a. 562 is the same as 5 hundreds, [ ] tens, and [ ] ones

b. 447 is the same as 2 hundreds, [ ] tens, and [ ] ones

c. 365 is the same as 1 hundred, [ ] tens, and [ ] ones

Common fractions: Adding mixed numbers (composing whole numbers)

Step In

The owner of a cafe has estimated there are about $1\frac{5}{8}$ gallons of strawberry ice cream in one container and $2\frac{6}{8}$ gallons of lemon ice cream in another.

What is the total amount of ice cream in the two containers?

Do you think that it is more or less than 4 gallons?

How could you figure it out?

I could count on from $2\frac{6}{8}$.

I could split each mixed number into wholes and fractions. I know that $\frac{5}{8} + \frac{6}{8}$ will be greater than $\frac{8}{8}$. What can I do about that total?

In a standard mixed number, the fractional part has a numerator that is less than the denominator.

How would you change the total to show a standard mixed number?

What will be the new total? Will it still represent the same amount? How do you know?

Step Up

1. Count on from one mixed number to calculate the total. Draw jumps on the number line to show your thinking.

a.

$2\frac{4}{5} + 1\frac{3}{5} = \boxed{}$

```
0       1       2       3       4       5
```

b.

$1\frac{5}{6} + 1\frac{4}{6} = \boxed{}$

```
0       1       2       3       4
```

2. Split each mixed number into whole numbers and fractions before adding. Then write the total. Show your thinking.

a.

$5 \frac{3}{4} + 2 \frac{2}{4} = \boxed{}$

b.

$3 \frac{6}{8} + 4 \frac{3}{8} = \boxed{}$

c.

$8 \frac{2}{6} + 4 \frac{5}{6} = \boxed{}$

d.

$6 \frac{4}{12} + 3 \frac{10}{12} = \boxed{}$

e.

$7 \frac{3}{5} + 4 \frac{3}{5} = \boxed{}$

f.

$2 \frac{6}{8} + 4 \frac{7}{8} = \boxed{}$

Step Ahead

Figure out which pairs of mixed numbers add to make a whole number and color them the same. Some mixed numbers do not have a match.

| $3 \frac{11}{12}$ | $2 \frac{3}{12}$ | $3 \frac{6}{12}$ | $1 \frac{7}{12}$ |

| $4 \frac{9}{12}$ | $4 \frac{1}{12}$ | $6 \frac{5}{12}$ | $5 \frac{4}{12}$ |

Step In

Damon went to the movies and bought a small box of popcorn.

At the start of the movie, the box was $\frac{7}{8}$ full.
By the end of the movie, Damon had eaten $\frac{5}{8}$ of the box.

How full was the box after the movie?

What equation could you write?

When you subtract fractions what happens to the numerator? What happens to the denominator?

$$\boxed{} - \boxed{} = \boxed{}$$

How could you show the difference on this number line?

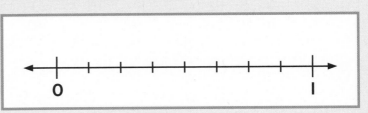

Ruby and her friend bought a box of popcorn to share. The box was full.
By the end of the movie, they had each eaten $\frac{3}{8}$ of the box.
How full was the box at the end of the movie? How could you calculate the amount?

Step Up

1. Draw and label jumps to match each equation.

a.
$$\frac{11}{6} - \frac{7}{6} = \frac{4}{6}$$

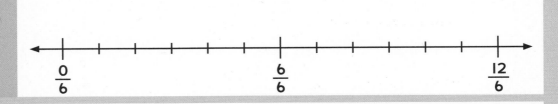

b.
$$\frac{13}{8} - \frac{4}{8} = \frac{9}{8}$$

c.
$$\frac{16}{4} - \frac{12}{4} = \frac{4}{4}$$

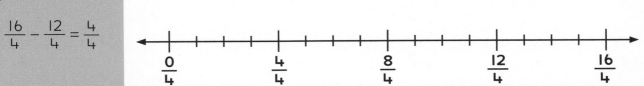

2. Use this number line to help you write the differences.

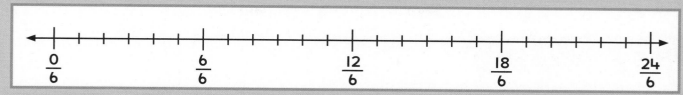

$$\frac{0}{6} \qquad \frac{6}{6} \qquad \frac{12}{6} \qquad \frac{18}{6} \qquad \frac{24}{6}$$

a. $\dfrac{15}{6} - \dfrac{4}{6} = \boxed{}$

b. $\boxed{} = \dfrac{20}{6} - \dfrac{8}{6}$

c. $\dfrac{17}{6} - \dfrac{2}{6} = \boxed{}$

d. $\boxed{} = \dfrac{23}{6} - \dfrac{9}{6}$

e. $\dfrac{21}{6} - \dfrac{16}{6} = \boxed{}$

f. $\boxed{} = \dfrac{18}{6} - 1$

3. Use what you know about subtracting fractions to calculate the difference between each pair of numbers.

a. $\dfrac{9}{10} \qquad \dfrac{4}{10}$

Difference $\boxed{}$

b. $\dfrac{15}{4} \qquad \dfrac{12}{4}$

Difference $\boxed{}$

c. $\dfrac{5}{8} \qquad \dfrac{23}{8}$

Difference $\boxed{}$

d. $1 \qquad \dfrac{3}{8}$

Difference $\boxed{}$

4. Write the missing fraction in each equation.

a. $\dfrac{11}{12} = \dfrac{18}{12} - \boxed{}$

b. $\dfrac{34}{8} - \boxed{} = \dfrac{26}{8}$

c. $\dfrac{2}{3} = \boxed{} - \dfrac{14}{3}$

Step Ahead   Complete each equation so the difference is **between 2 and 3**.

a. $\dfrac{16}{4} - \boxed{} = \boxed{}$

b. $\dfrac{25}{6} - \boxed{} = \boxed{}$

c. $\dfrac{20}{8} - \boxed{} = \boxed{}$

d. $\dfrac{22}{4} - \boxed{} = \boxed{}$

Working Space

Think and Solve

a. The product of two numbers is 63. The sum of the two numbers is 16.

What is the difference between the two numbers? Show your thinking.

b. The difference between two prime numbers is 14.
The sum of the two numbers is 20.
What is the product of the two numbers?
Show your thinking on page 280.

Words at Work   Look at these three numbers. Write how they are the similar, and how they are different. $\frac{22}{4}$ $\frac{11}{2}$ $5\frac{1}{2}$

I. Use the standard addition algorithm to calculate the total.

a.

```
    3  0  7  5
    1  6  4  2
+   2  1  1  5
_____
```

b.

```
    2  4  1  5
    2  6  0  5  1
+  3  2  7  1  6
_____
```

c.

```
    4  2  0  0  1
    1  6  9  5  0
+  3  4  5  0  7
_____
```

FROM 4.2.6

2. Each large rectangle is one whole. Shade parts using different colors to show each fraction. Then write the total fraction that is shaded.

a.

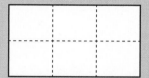

$\frac{2}{6} + \frac{3}{6} = $ _____

b.

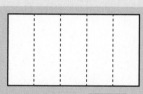

$\frac{2}{5} + \frac{1}{5} = $ _____

c.

$\frac{3}{10} + \frac{4}{10} = $ _____

d.

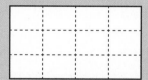

$\frac{7}{12} + \frac{3}{12} = $ _____

e.

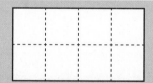

$\frac{4}{8} + \frac{2}{8} = $ _____

f.

$\frac{4}{6} + \frac{1}{6} = $ _____

FROM 4.7.5

Preparing for Module 8

Each large shape is one whole. Color parts to show the total. Then complete the equation.

$\frac{1}{6} + \frac{1}{6} + \frac{1}{6} + \frac{1}{6} + \frac{1}{6} + \frac{1}{6} + \frac{1}{6} + \frac{1}{6} + \frac{1}{6} = $ _____

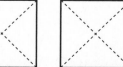

$\frac{1}{4} + \frac{1}{4} + \frac{1}{4} + \frac{1}{4} + \frac{1}{4} + \frac{1}{4} = $ _____

Step In

One bag of bananas weighs $5\frac{3}{4}$ pounds.
Another bag weighs $3\frac{2}{4}$ pounds.

How could you calculate the difference in mass between the two bags?

I would start with $5\frac{3}{4}$ and take away $3\frac{2}{4}$ in smaller jumps. One jump would be 3 and the next jump would be $\frac{2}{4}$.

When I add mixed numbers, I add the whole numbers and fractions separately, then combine their totals. I think this will work for subtraction too.

How was addition used to calculate the difference on this number line?

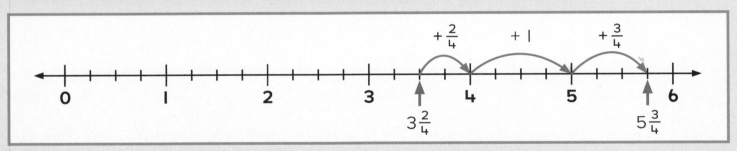

How could subtraction be used to find the difference?

Step Up

1. Calculate the difference. Draw jumps on the number line to show your thinking.

a.

$3\frac{4}{6} - 1\frac{2}{6} = \boxed{}$

b.

$4\frac{4}{5} - 3\frac{3}{5} = \boxed{}$

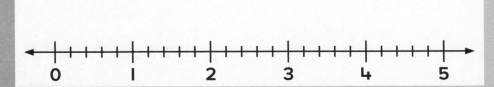

2. Calculate the difference. Draw jumps on the number line to show your thinking.

a.

$3\frac{2}{4} - 1\frac{1}{4} = \boxed{}$

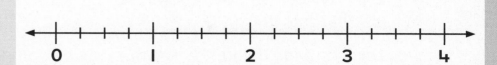

b.

$2\frac{6}{8} - 1\frac{3}{8} = \boxed{}$

3. Calculate the difference. Show your thinking.

a.

$6\frac{7}{8} - 2\frac{4}{8} = \boxed{}$

b.

$5\frac{4}{10} - 4\frac{2}{10} = \boxed{}$

c.

$6\frac{10}{12} - 1\frac{7}{12} = \boxed{}$

d.

$10\frac{5}{6} - 2\frac{3}{6} = \boxed{}$

e.

$9\frac{8}{12} - 8\frac{2}{12} = \boxed{}$

f.

$6\frac{7}{10} - 1\frac{7}{10} = \boxed{}$

Step Ahead   Write the missing numbers on this trail.

$\boxed{4\frac{1}{12}} \rightarrow \left\langle +3\frac{9}{12} \right\rangle \rightarrow \boxed{} \rightarrow \left\langle -2\frac{7}{12} \right\rangle \rightarrow \boxed{} \rightarrow \left\langle +5\frac{8}{12} \right\rangle \rightarrow \boxed{}$

Step In

Andrew has two pet lizards. One is $3\frac{4}{8}$ inches long and the other is $1\frac{7}{8}$ inches long.

How could you figure out the difference between their lengths?

Laura figured it out as shown on the right.
What did she do to make the subtraction easier?

How could you use addition to help you calculate the difference?

Look at the number lines below.

What is the same about the two methods shown?
What is different?

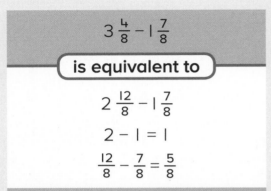

$$3\frac{4}{8} - 1\frac{7}{8}$$

is equivalent to

$$2\frac{12}{8} - 1\frac{7}{8}$$

$$2 - 1 = 1$$

$$\frac{12}{8} - \frac{7}{8} = \frac{5}{8}$$

The difference $1\frac{5}{8}$ inches.

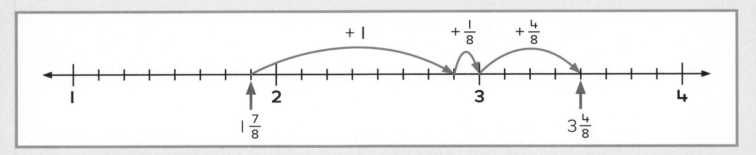

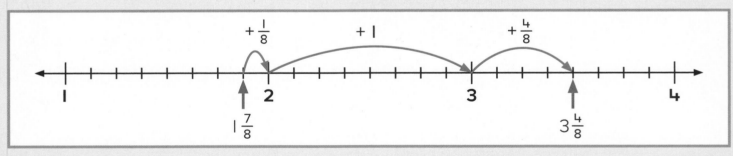

Step Up

1. Calculate the difference. Draw jumps on the number line to show your thinking.

$$3\frac{2}{6} - 2\frac{5}{6} = \boxed{}$$

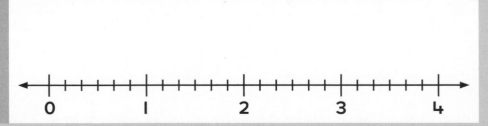

© ORIGO Education

2. Calculate the difference. Draw jumps on the number line to show your thinking.

a.

$5\frac{1}{3} - 2\frac{2}{3} =$

```
 ◄──┼┼┼┼┼┼┼┼┼┼┼┼┼┼┼┼┼┼──►
    0   1   2   3   4   5   6
```

b.

$4\frac{1}{5} - 3\frac{3}{5} =$

```
 ◄──┼┼┼┼┼┼┼┼┼┼┼┼┼┼┼┼┼┼──►
    0   1   2   3   4   5
```

3. Calculate the difference. Show your thinking.

a.

$7\frac{1}{6} - 2\frac{4}{6} =$

b.

$= 6\frac{2}{5} - 5\frac{4}{5}$

c.

$9\frac{3}{10} - 4\frac{3}{10} =$

d.

$= 14\frac{2}{8} - 1\frac{3}{8}$

e.

$16\frac{4}{12} - 11\frac{9}{12} =$

f.

$= 5 - 3\frac{6}{8}$

Step Ahead

Look at these related equations.

$4 + 2 = 6$ $2 + 4 = 6$ $6 - 2 = 4$ $6 - 4 = 2$

Each describes the same two parts (4 and 2) that make a total (6). Write the related equations for this equation.

$3\frac{7}{8} + 2\frac{4}{8} = 6\frac{3}{8}$

© ORIGO Education

Computation Practice   What do you give a seasick monster?

★ Complete the equations. Find each product in the grid below and cross out the letter above. Then write the remaining letters at the bottom of the page.

$3 \times 46 = $ ____

$53 \times 4 = $ ____

$6 \times 48 = $ ____

$54 \times 7 = $ ____

$6 \times 54 = $ ____

$49 \times 6 = $ ____

$47 \times 5 = $ ____

$63 \times 7 = $ ____

$5 \times 63 = $ ____

$39 \times 8 = $ ____

$5 \times 36 = $ ____

$6 \times 64 = $ ____

$7 \times 47 = $ ____

$4 \times 48 = $ ____

$74 \times 5 = $ ____

$4 \times 36 = $ ____

$3 \times 76 = $ ____

$54 \times 3 = $ ____

$6 \times 28 = $ ____

$65 \times 3 = $ ____

L	O	L	L	I	E	S	O	D	A
138	324	202	212	168	180	288	421	162	378
T	A	B	L	E	T	S	O	F	T
344	144	235	195	294	228	170	334	302	315
D	R	I	N	K	G	L	O	O	M
384	364	192	441	312	329	370	148	172	185

Write the letters in order from the ✳ to the bottom-right corner.

© ORIGO Education

Ongoing Practice

1. Draw a line to connect each time to the correct clock.

| 25 minutes past 5 | 7:10 | 10 past 7 | 5:25 | 20 minutes to 2 | 8 minutes to 3 | 1:40 |

FROM 3.2.8

2. Add these mixed numbers. Show your thinking on the number line.

a.

$2\frac{1}{4} + 2\frac{2}{4} = $ ☐

```
<──┼──┼──┼──┼──┼──┼──┼──┼──┼──┼──┼──┼──┼──┼──┼──┼──┼──┼──┼──┼──>
   0           1           2           3           4           5
```

FROM 4.7.6

b.

$2\frac{3}{8} + 1\frac{4}{8} = $ ☐

```
<──┼──┼──┼──┼──┼──┼──┼──┼──┼──┼──┼──┼──┼──┼──┼──┼──┼──┼──┼──┼──┼──┼──┼──┼──>
   0           1           2           3           4
```

Preparing for Module 8

Draw jumps to show how to count to reach the fraction. Then write an equation to match the jumps you made.

a.

$\frac{3}{4}$

```
<──┼──────────┼──────────┼──────────┼──────────┼──>
   0                                            1
```

b.

$\frac{2}{3}$

```
<──┼──────────┼──────────┼──────────┼──>
   0                                  1
```

© ORIGO Education

ORIGO Stepping Stones · Grade 4 · 7.10

273 ◆

Step In

Nathan uses a watering can to pour $3\frac{3}{4}$ liters of water onto his seedlings. They are in a garden bed that is $5\frac{3}{4}$ feet long. Afterward, the watering can still has $4\frac{3}{4}$ liters of water in it.

How much water was in the watering can at the start?
How would you calculate the answer?

Which information is important?

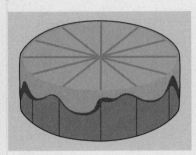

Two identical cakes have been baked for a big party. Each cake is cut into twelfths. Halfway through the party, $\frac{3}{12}$ of one cake has been eaten. The other cake has 4 pieces missing and 5 people are standing near it.

How much cake was left?
Which operations will you use to calculate the amount?

Step Up

1. Write an equation to represent each problem. Use a letter to represent the unknown amount. You do not need to calculate the final answer.

a. Bella and Elvis are cats. Bella weighs $4\frac{1}{10}$ kilograms. The total mass of the cats is $9\frac{7}{10}$ kilograms. How much does Elvis weigh?

b. A bucket holds $3\frac{1}{2}$ gallons of water. $1\frac{1}{2}$ gallons is used for watering lettuce and $\frac{1}{2}$ gallon is poured on carrots. How much water is left?

c. A builder cut $2\frac{7}{8}$ inches off a length of lumber. The piece left was $5\frac{3}{8}$ inches long. How long was the piece of lumber at the start?

d. Peta is visiting her dad. It took $2\frac{1}{4}$ hours to get there. It usually takes $1\frac{3}{4}$ hours. How much later than usual did she arrive?

2. Solve each problem. Show your thinking.

a. Oscar cuts 5 oranges into sixths for a picnic. Afterward, there is only $\frac{4}{6}$ of an orange left. How much orange has been eaten?

[   ] oranges

b. Two statues are being packed into a box. One weighs $7\frac{3}{8}$ lb and the other weighs $9\frac{4}{8}$ lb. What is their total mass?

[   ] pounds

c. Two full 2-liter bottles of water are placed in a fridge. After four days, one bottle is half full. The other has $1\frac{3}{10}$ liters left in it. How much water is there in total?

[   ] L

d. A chain is $8\frac{5}{12}$ feet long. It is joined to another chain so the total length is $10\frac{9}{12}$ feet. How long is the extra piece of chain?

[   ] ft

Step Ahead

Write a subtraction word problem that involves mixed numbers and common fractions.

_____

_____

_____

_____

Common fractions: Interpreting line plots to solve word problems

Step In

Two friends are training for a triathlon.
The line plots show the distances they have run.

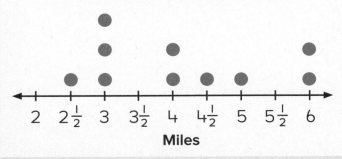

Running Distance (Nicole)

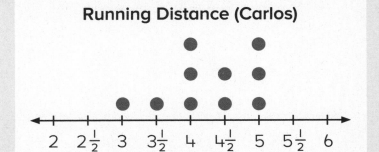

Running Distance (Carlos)

How many times did each person go running?

Who ran the greatest distance **in one run**?

What was the most common distance that each person ran?

How would you calculate the **total** distance that each person ran?

I added the whole numbers and then the fractions.
It helps to record each distance in a list.

Step Up

I. Your teacher will give you a support page. Draw ● on the line plot below to show the distance that Dixon cycled each day.

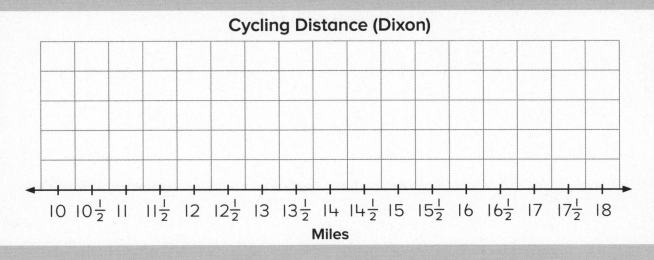

Cycling Distance (Dixon)

10 10½ 11 11½ 12 12½ 13 13½ 14 14½ 15 15½ 16 16½ 17 17½ 18

Miles

2. Look at the support page. Draw ● on the line plot below to show the distance that Stella cycled each day.

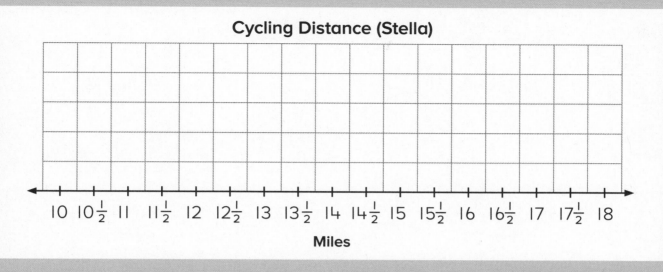

Cycling Distance (Stella)

$10 \quad 10\frac{1}{2} \quad 11 \quad 11\frac{1}{2} \quad 12 \quad 12\frac{1}{2} \quad 13 \quad 13\frac{1}{2} \quad 14 \quad 14\frac{1}{2} \quad 15 \quad 15\frac{1}{2} \quad 16 \quad 16\frac{1}{2} \quad 17 \quad 17\frac{1}{2} \quad 18$

Miles

3. Use the line plots in Questions 1 and 2 to answer these questions.

   a. How many times did each person go cycling?

   b. Who cycled the greatest distance in one ride?

   c. What distance did Dixon cycle most often? _____ miles

   d. What is the difference between the greatest and least distance that each person cycled?

   Dixon _____

   Stella _____

Step Ahead

Use the line plot in Question 2. Calculate the total distance Stella cycled. Show your thinking.

_____ miles

Think and Solve

THINK TANK

Clues

- Shape B weighs half as much as Shape A.

- Shape A weighs 200 kg.

- Shape C is lighter than Shape B.

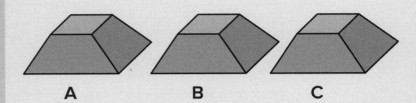

A   B   C

How could you describe the mass of Shape C?

Shape C is _____

Words at Work

Write a subtraction word problem that involves mixed numbers. Then write how you would find the solution.

_____
_____
_____
_____
_____
_____
_____
_____
_____
_____
_____

Ongoing Practice

1. Write these times using **minutes to**.

a.

_____ minutes
to _____

b.

_____ minutes
to _____

c.

_____ minutes
to _____

d.

_____ minutes
to _____

2. Use this number line to help you write the differences.

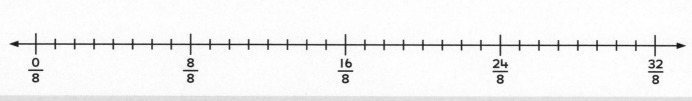

a.

$$\frac{20}{8} - \frac{5}{8} = \boxed{}$$

b.

$$\boxed{} = \frac{17}{8} - \frac{11}{8}$$

c.

$$\frac{27}{8} - \frac{10}{8} = \boxed{}$$

d.

$$\boxed{} = \frac{12}{8} - \frac{7}{8}$$

e.

$$\frac{31}{8} - \frac{20}{8} = \boxed{}$$

f.

$$\boxed{} = \frac{18}{8} - 2$$

Preparing for Module 8

Color the tens part red and the ones part blue. Then write each product. Add the two partial products, and write the total.

3 × 36

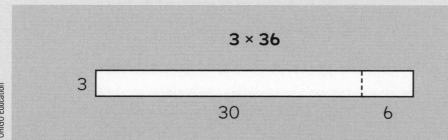

3   30   6

3 × _____ = _____

3 × _____ = _____

Total _____

Step In   **What do you know about this rectangle?**

5 ft   Area is 45 ft²

?

How can you calculate the length of the rectangle?

Write two equations you could use to help you.

☐ × ☐ = ☐   ☐ ÷ ☐ = ☐

What do you know about this square?

What thinking would you use to calculate the length of the unknown side?

? Area is 36 m²

6 m

What equations could you write?

_____   _____

Step Up   1. Complete the two equations you could use to calculate the unknown dimension. Then label the diagram.

a.

4 yd   Area is 28 yd²

☐ yd

4 × ___ = 28

28 ÷ 4 = ___

b.

Area is 48 ft²

 ft

8 ft

8 × ___ = 48

48 ÷ 8 = ___

© ORIGO Education

2. Complete each of these.

a.

7 m   **Area is 63 m²**

☐____ m

____ × ____ = ____

____ ÷ ____ = ____

b.

Area is 8 in²   ☐____ in

8 in

____ × ____ = ____

____ ÷ ____ = ____

c.

6 cm   **Area is 42 cm²**

☐____ cm

____ × ____ = ____

____ ÷ ____ = ____

d.

Area is 27 yd²   3 yd

☐____ yd

____ × ____ = ____

____ ÷ ____ = ____

3. Write the missing number in each fact.

a. $36 \div 9 = $ ☐

b. $4 = $ ☐ $\div 8$

c. $1 = $ ☐ $\div 9$

d. $35 \div $ ☐ $= 7$

e. $54 \div $ ☐ $= 9$

f. ☐ $\div 9 = 9$

g. $30 \div $ ☐ $= 5$

h. $9 = $ ☐ $\div 2$

Step Ahead

Write three pairs of possible dimensions for a rectangle that has an area of 600 ft².

☐ × ☐ = 600 ft²

☐ × ☐ = 600 ft²

☐ × ☐ = 600 ft²

Working Space

© ORIGO Education

Step In   Three friends share the cost of this gift.

How can you calculate the amount that each person will pay?

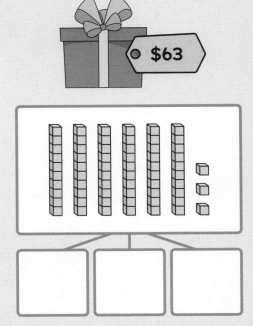

William uses a sharing strategy.

What do the blocks at the top of the chart represent?

What steps will he follow?

What amount will each person pay? How do you know?

What division equation could you write?

Daniela uses a different strategy. She follows these steps.

Step 1	Step 2	Step 3
She draws a rectangle to show the problem. The length of one side becomes the unknown value.	She partitions the rectangle into two parts so that it is easier to divide by 3.	She thinks: $3 \times 20 = 60$ $3 \times 1 = 3$ then $20 + 1 = 21$

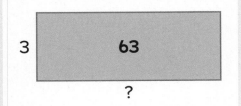 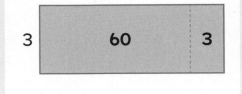 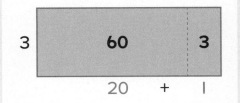

Why did she split the rectangle into two parts?

Why did she choose the numbers 60 and 3?

Why did she add 20 and 1?

I will call the amount that each person pays **A**. To find the amount, William thinks $63 \div 3 = A$, and Daniela thinks $3 \times A = 63$.

How could you use these strategies to calculate $96 \div 3$?

1. These rectangles have been partitioned to make it easier to divide. Write the missing numbers. Then complete the equation.

a.

86 ÷ 2 = _____

| 2 | **80** | **6** |

_____ + _____

b.

69 ÷ 3 = _____

| 3 | **60** | **9** |

_____ + _____

c.

62 ÷ 2 = _____

| 2 | **60** | **2** |

_____ + _____

d.

48 ÷ 4 = _____

| 4 | **40** | **8** |

_____ + _____

2. Inside each rectangle, write numbers that are easier to divide. Divide the two parts then complete the equation.

a.

93 ÷ 3 = _____

| 3 | ☐ _____ | ☐ _____ |

_____ + _____

b.

77 ÷ 7 = _____

| 7 | ☐ _____ | ☐ _____ |

_____ + _____

Break each number into parts that you can easily **divide by 3**.

a.

915

b.

612

c.

396

Computation Practice   Which spiders have the shortest legs?

★ For each division card, use a ruler to draw a straight line to the correct quotient. The line will pass through a number and a letter. Write each letter above its matching number at the bottom of the page. Some quotients are used more than once.

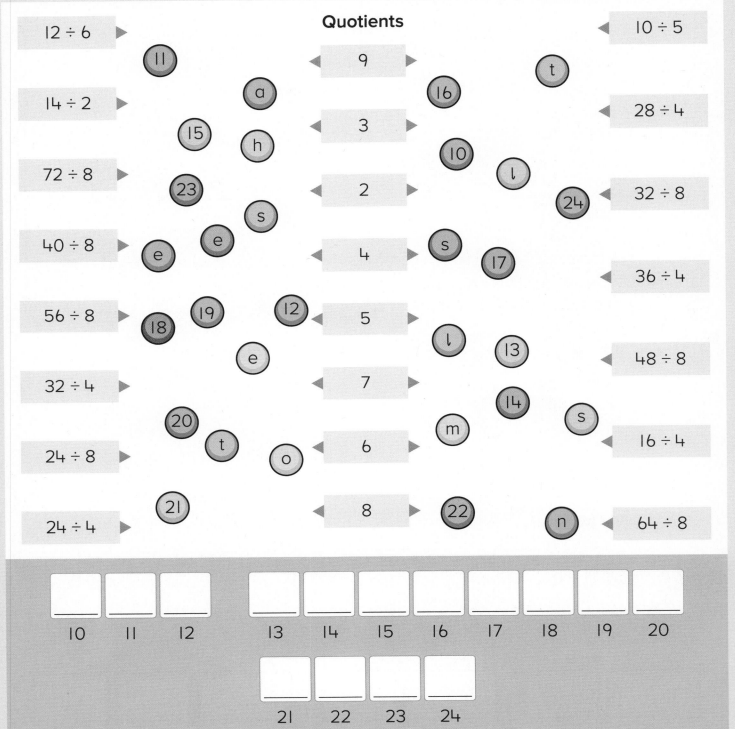

10	11	12	13	14	15	16	17	18	19	20

21	22	23	24

Ongoing Practice

1. This table shows the school dance ticket sales for four days. Complete the graph to show the results.

Day	Total Sales
Monday	35
Tuesday	40
Wednesday	60
Thursday	15

Ticket Sales   ☐ means 10 tickets

Monday							
Tuesday							
Wednesday							
Thursday							

2. Each rectangle has been partitioned to make it easier to divide. Write the missing numbers. Then complete the equation.

a.

$64 \div 2 =$ _____

2 | **60** ┊ **4**

 **30** + _____

b.

$93 \div 3 =$ _____

3 | **90** ┊ **3**

_____ + _____

c.

$88 \div 4 =$ _____

4 | **80** ┊ **8**

_____ + _____

d.

$84 \div 2 =$ _____

2 | **80** ┊ **4**

_____ + _____

Preparing for Module 9

On each number line, the distance from 0 to 1 is one whole. Find each fraction on the number line. Then write <, =, or > to make each statement true.

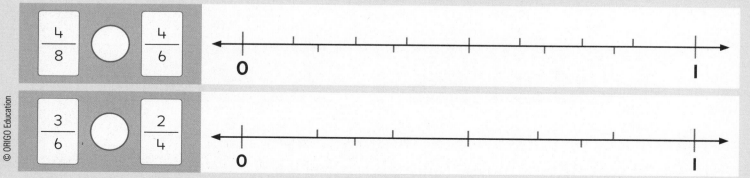

$\dfrac{4}{8}$ ◯ $\dfrac{4}{6}$

0 ———————————————— 1

$\dfrac{3}{6}$ ◯ $\dfrac{2}{4}$

0 ———————————————— 1

Step In

How can you calculate the length of this rectangle?

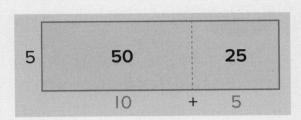

5 ft   Area is 75 ft²

?

I know that 5 × 10 = 50.
That leaves 25 left over.

Sumi partitioned the rectangle like this.

Why did she choose the numbers 50 and 25?

What is the length of the unknown side?

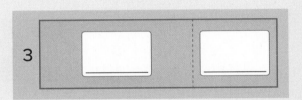

5 | 50 | 25
10 + 5

Partition this rectangle so that it is easier to calculate 45 ÷ 3.

Write numbers inside the rectangle to show the parts.

How did you break 45 into two parts?

How could this help you calculate 45 ÷ 3?

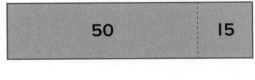

3 | ☐ | ☐

Step Up

1. These rectangles have been partitioned to make it easier to divide. Write the missing numbers. Then complete the equation.

a.

56 ÷ 4 = _____

4 | 40 | 16

_____ + _____

b.

65 ÷ 5 = _____

5 | 50 | 15

_____ + _____

c.

72 ÷ 6 = _____

6 | 60 | 12

_____ + _____

d.

84 ÷ 7 = _____

7 | 70 | 14

_____ + _____

2. Inside each rectangle, write numbers that are easier to divide.
Divide the two parts then complete the equation.

a.
$90 \div 6 =$ ___

6

___ + ___

b.
$51 \div 3 =$ ___

3

___ + ___

c.
$60 \div 4 =$ ___

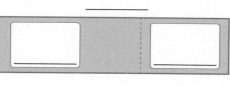

4

___ + ___

d.
$91 \div 7 =$ ___

7

___ + ___

3. Break each starting number into parts that you can easily divide.
Then complete the equations.

a.
$85 \div 5 =$ ☐

(is the same value as)

___ $\div 5$ plus ___ $\div 5 =$ ___

b.
$48 \div 3 =$ ☐

(is the same value as)

___ $\div 3$ plus ___ $\div 3 =$ ___

c.
$96 \div 8 =$ ☐

(is the same value as)

___ $\div 8$ plus ___ $\div 8 =$ ___

d.
$84 \div 6 =$ ☐

(is the same value as)

___ $\div 6$ plus ___ $\div 6 =$ ___

Step Ahead Use the same thinking to complete these equations.

a.
$42 \div 3 =$ ☐

b.
$95 \div 5 =$ ☐

c.
$84 \div 4 =$ ☐

d.
$102 \div 6 =$ ☐

© ORIGO Education

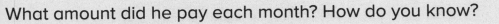

Step In David paid for this laptop in three monthly payments. He paid the same amount each month.

$639

What amount did he pay each month? How do you know?

I would break 639 into parts that are easier to divide.

Describe how this rectangle has been partitioned.

What is special about the numbers 600, 30, and 9?

What amount does David pay each month?

| 3 | 600 | 30 | 9 |

200 + 10 + 3

Trina's laptop was $546. She paid the same amount each month for six months.

How can you calculate the amount she paid each month?

Felipe uses this diagram to break 546 into parts that are easier to divide by 6.

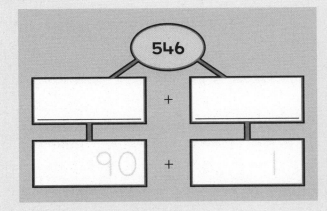

546

+

90   +

Complete the equations to calculate the amount that Trina paid each month.

$540 \div 6 = \boxed{}$

How do the equations match the numbers used in the diagram?

$6 \div 6 = \boxed{}$

Use the same strategy to calculate 279 ÷ 3.

$546 \div 6 = \boxed{}$

1. These rectangles have been partitioned to make it easier to divide. Divide each part then complete the equation.

a.

$606 \div 6 =$ _____

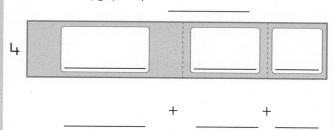

6 | **600** | **6**

_____ + _____

b.

$963 \div 3 =$ _____

3 | **900** | **60** | **3**

_____ + _____ + _____

c.

$484 \div 4 =$ _____

4 | _____ | _____ | _____

_____ + _____ + _____

d.

$530 \div 5 =$ _____

5 | _____ | _____

_____ + _____

2. Estimate each answer. Then calculate the exact quotient. Show your thinking.

$24 \div 6 = 4$
Dividend   Divisor   Quotient

a.

Estimate _____

$742 \div 7 =$ _____

b.

Estimate _____

$693 \div 3 =$ _____

c.

Estimate _____

$630 \div 6 =$ _____

Write the missing numbers. You can make notes on page 318.

a.

_____ $\div 4 = 132$

b.

_____ $\div 6 = 104$

© ORIGO Education

Think and Solve What is the number on the back of Jude's shirt? ⬚

- It is less than 7 × 9.

- It is greater than 6 × 8.

- It is a multiple of 5.

- When you divide it by 7, you get a remainder of 1.

Words at Work

Imagine another student was away from school when you were learning about the partial-quotients strategy for division. Write in words how you would explain the strategy to them.

_____

_____

_____

_____

_____

_____

_____

_____

_____

_____

_____

_____

Ongoing Practice

1. Use the graph to answer the questions.

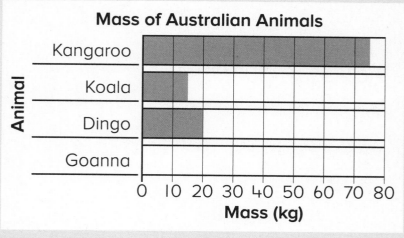

Mass of Australian Animals

Animal: Kangaroo, Koala, Dingo, Goanna
Mass (kg): 0 10 20 30 40 50 60 70 80

a. Color the graph to show that the goanna's mass is 10 kg.

b. What is the difference in mass between the kangaroo and koala?

_____ kg

c. How much more does the dingo weigh than the goanna?

_____ kg

FROM 3.6.10

2. Break each starting number into parts that you can easily divide. Then complete the equations.

a. $45 \div 3 = \boxed{}$

is the same value as

_____ $\div 3$ plus _____ $\div 3 =$ _____

b. $65 \div 5 = \boxed{}$

is the same value as

_____ $\div 5$ plus _____ $\div 5 =$ _____

c. $72 \div 6 = \boxed{}$

is the same value as

_____ $\div 6$ plus _____ $\div 6 =$ _____

d. $84 \div 7 = \boxed{}$

is the same value as

_____ $\div 7$ plus _____ $\div 7 =$ _____

FROM 4.8.3

Preparing for Module 9

Circle the fraction that is greater in each pair.

a. $\frac{1}{2}$ $\frac{1}{3}$

b. $\frac{1}{8}$ $\frac{1}{3}$

c. $\frac{1}{4}$ $\frac{1}{2}$

d. $\frac{1}{4}$ $\frac{1}{8}$

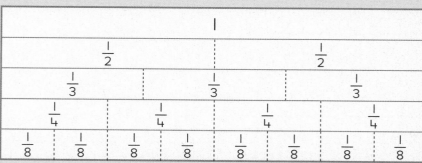

© ORIGO Education

Step In

Samantha paid $453 to buy three concert tickets. Each ticket costs the same amount.

How could you estimate the price of each ticket?

> I thought of a number that will give me 450 when multiplied by 3.

What numbers could you write in this diagram to help calculate the exact price of each ticket?

How do the parts in this diagram help you divide by 3?

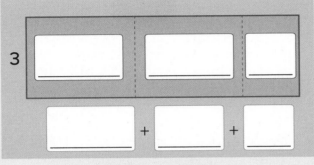

Jamal paid $296 to buy four theme park tickets. Each ticket costs the same amount.

How could you calculate the price of each ticket?

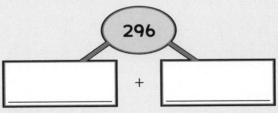

> You could break 296 into two parts that are easier to divide by 4.

What is the price of each ticket? How do you know?

How do the two parts help you divide by 4?

Complete the equations to calculate the price.

Use this strategy to calculate 258 ÷ 3.

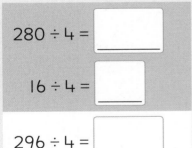

$280 \div 4 =$ ☐

$16 \div 4 =$ ☐

$296 \div 4 =$ ☐

Step Up

1. Break each number into parts that you can easily divide by 4.

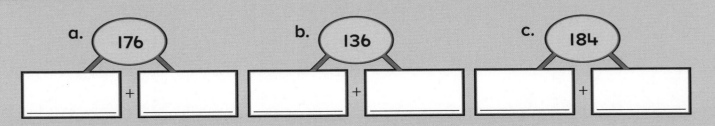

a. 176

☐ + ☐

b. 136

☐ + ☐

c. 184

☐ + ☐

2. Write equations to calculate each quotient.

a.
265 ÷ 5 = _____

250 ÷ 5 = _____

15 ÷ 5 = _____

b.
364 ÷ 4 = _____

320 ÷ 4 = _____

_____ ÷ 4 = _____

c.
108 ÷ 3 = _____

90 ÷ 3 = _____

_____ ÷ 3 = _____

d. 342 ÷ 6 = _____

e. 126 ÷ 3 = _____

f. 496 ÷ 8 = _____

g. 426 ÷ 3 = _____

h. 786 ÷ 6 = _____

i. 568 ÷ 4 = _____

3. Solve each problem. Show your thinking.

a. A new pier is 492 ft long. It is 3 times as long as the old pier. What is the length of the old pier?

_____ ft

b. 112 stickers are arranged in an array of 8 columns. How many rows of stickers are there?

_____ rows

Step Ahead

Calculate the cost of buying a two-day pass for each theme park. Then circle the theme park that is the least expensive.

2-DAY PASS REPTILE PARK

5 passes cost $480

2-DAY PASS DREAM LAND

4 passes cost $336

2-DAY PASS OCEAN WORLD

3 passes cost $324

Step In

The Hornets have **6,936** members.
They have three times as many members as the Wild Cats.

How many members do the Wild Cats have?

> There must be more than 2,000 members because 6,000 ÷ 3 = 2,000.

Allison wrote these equations to calculate the answer.
Write the missing quotients.

How did she break 6,936 into parts that are easier to divide by 3?

Can you think of another way to break 6,936 into parts?

$6{,}000 \div 3 = $ ____

$900 \div 3 = $ ____

$30 \div 3 = $ ____

$6 \div 3 = $ ____

$6{,}936 \div 3 = $ ____

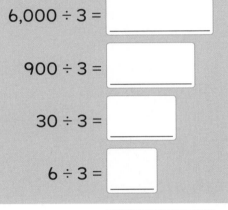

> I would group the tens and ones together. 36 ÷ 3 is easy to calculate.

Step Up

I. Break each number into parts you can easily **divide by 4**.

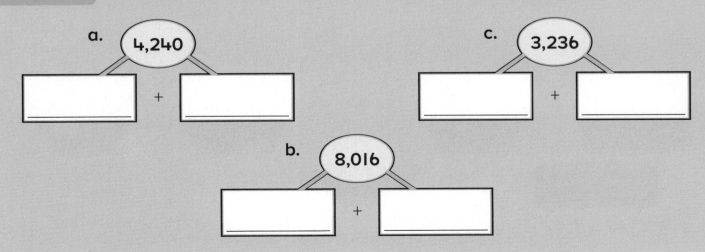

a. 4,240

____ + ____

c. 3,236

____ + ____

b. 8,016

____ + ____

2. Write equations to calculate each quotient.

a. 3,603 ÷ 3 = _____

3,000 ÷ 3 = _____

600 ÷ 3 = _____

3 ÷ 3 = _____

b. 8,032 ÷ 4 = _____

8,000 ÷ 4 = _____

32 ÷ 4 = _____

c. 3,930 ÷ 3 = _____

3,000 ÷ 3 = _____

900 ÷ 3 = _____

30 ÷ 3 = _____

d. 4,824 ÷ 4 = _____

e. 9,036 ÷ 3 = _____

f. 5,050 ÷ 5 = _____

g. 6,036 ÷ 6 = _____

h. 5,525 ÷ 5 = _____

i. 1,815 ÷ 3 = _____

Step Ahead   Write the missing numbers.

a. [ ] ÷ 4 = 2,106

b. [ ] ÷ 3 = 2,307

Working Space

Computation Practice   **What do you get if you cross a porcupine with a giraffe?**

★ Complete the equations. Then find each total in the puzzle below and color its matching letter red.

326 + 218 = _____

336 + 258 = _____

463 + 108 = _____

326 + 148 = _____

235 + 346 = _____

218 + 356 = _____

338 + 257 = _____

436 + 227 = _____

369 + 423 = _____

417 + 105 = _____

358 + 214 = _____

337 + 146 = _____

248 + 537 = _____

148 + 726 = _____

265 + 326 = _____

116 + 237 = _____

528 + 259 = _____

648 + 255 = _____

359 + 237 = _____

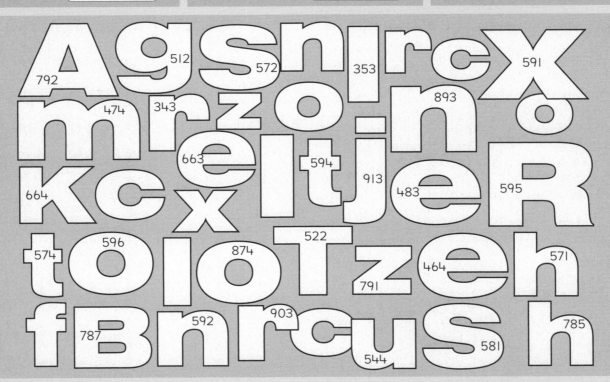

1. Estimate each difference. Then use the standard subtraction algorithm to calculate the exact difference.

a. Estimate

Th	H	T	O
7	5	0	6
− 1	3	8	4

b. Estimate

TTh	Th	H	T	O
2	6	0	7	9
−	8	5	1	6

c. Estimate

TTh	Th	H	T	O
1	0	3	8	5
−	6	7	2	1

2. These rectangles have been partitioned to make them easier to divide. Divide each part then complete the equation.

a.

448 ÷ 8 = _____

8 | 400 | 48

_____ + _____

b.

693 ÷ 3 = _____

3 | 600 | 90 | 3

_____ + _____ + _____

Use the number line to help you write equivalent fractions.

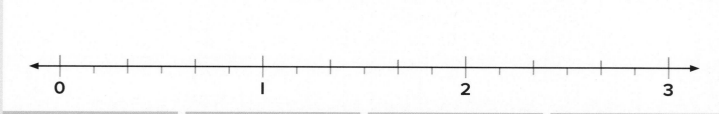

0   1   2   3

a.

$\frac{1}{3} =$ _____

b.

_____ $= \frac{10}{6}$

c.

$\frac{7}{3} =$ _____

d.

_____ $= \frac{16}{6}$

Step In A beachside condo costs **$5,236** to rent for four weeks.

What is the price of one week?

Would it cost more or less than $1,000 a week?
How do you know?

Sofia wrote these equations to calculate the price.
Write the quotients.

How did she break 5,236 into parts that are easier to divide by 4?

What is another way to break 5,236 into parts?

$4,000 \div 4 =$ ☐

$1,200 \div 4 =$ ☐

$36 \div 4 =$ ☐

$5,236 \div 4 =$ ☐

A smaller cabin costs $1,620 for four weeks.
What is the price of one week?

You could break 1,620 into parts that are easier to divide by 4. This diagram shows you how.

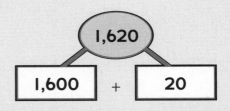

$1,600 \div 4 =$ ☐

$20 \div 4 =$ ☐

Complete the equations to show the price of one week.

$1,620 \div 4 =$ ☐

Step Up 1. Break each number into parts that you can easily **divide by 5**.

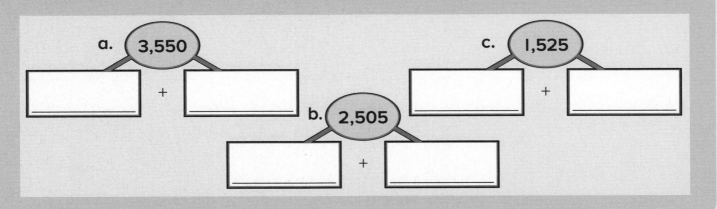

a. 3,550   ☐ + ☐

b. 2,505   ☐ + ☐

c. 1,525   ☐ + ☐

2. Write equations to calculate each quotient.

a.
$1,720 \div 4 =$ _____

$1,600 \div 4 =$ _____

$120 \div 4 =$ _____

b.
$1,659 \div 3 =$ _____

$1,500 \div 3 =$ _____

_____ $\div 3 =$ _____

_____ $\div 3 =$ _____

c.
$1,926 \div 6 =$ _____

$1,800 \div 6 =$ _____

_____ $\div 6 =$ _____

_____ $\div 6 =$ _____

3. Estimate each quotient in your head. Then calculate the exact quotient.

a.
$5,612 \div 4 =$ _____

b.
$8,407 \div 7 =$ _____

c.
$7,830 \div 6 =$ _____

4. Solve each problem. Show your thinking.

a. 3 families share the cost of renting a condo. It costs $2,040 for 7 days. What amount does each family pay?

$ _____

b. 3,245 park tickets are sold on Saturday. This is 5 times as many tickets that were sold on Monday. How many tickets sold on Monday?

_____ tickets

Step Ahead   Circle the numbers that you can divide **equally** by 4.

| 3,216 | 4,810 | 1,720 | 5,204 | 5,642 |

Step In

TAKE HOME TODAY!
Buy Now - Pay Later

$1,350

$786

$486

$85

Imagine you buy one of these items and pay for it over several months.

How would the store calculate the amount you need to pay each month?

Imagine you buy the television and pay equal monthly amounts over six months.

How much would you pay each month?

How could you break $786 into parts that are easy to divide by 6?

Step Up

I. Use the prices above. Calculate the equal monthly payments for these items. Show your thinking.

a. 5 monthly payments

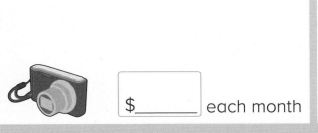

$_____ each month

b. 6 monthly payments

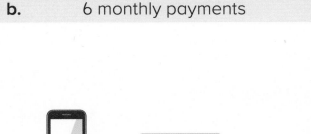

$_____ each month

2. Solve each problem. Show your thinking.

a. A spreadsheet has 18 rows and 15 columns. Paul shades every fifth cell. How many cells are shaded?

_____ cells

b. A sheet of cardboard is 25 inches wide and 30 inches long. The cardboard is cut into 3 equal pieces. What is the area of each piece?

_____ in²

c. There are 25 boxes of calculators with 50 calculators in each box. The calculators are shared equally among 5 schools. How many calculators are given to each school?

_____ calculators

d. Name tags are printed for a conference. There are 2 columns of 6 tags on each sheet. How many sheets are needed for 1,260 name tags?

_____ sheets

Step Ahead Calculate the monthly payments for each phone. Then draw a ✔ beside the plan that you would choose.

A

$520

paid over 8 months

$_____ each month

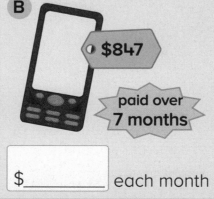

B

$847

paid over 7 months

$_____ each month

C

$635

paid over 5 months

$_____ each month

© ORIGO Education

Think and Solve   A, B, C, and D are whole numbers.

Clues

$A \times B = 56$
$B - A = 1$
$A + B = C$
$C \div 3 = D$

Whole numbers are 0, 1, 2, 3, 4, 5, and so on.

Use the clues to write the missing number in this equation.

$(D + C) \times (B + A) = \boxed{}$

Words at Work   These math terms are related to multiplication and division. Write the meaning of each.

a. partition a number

b. dividend

c. quotient

Ongoing Practice

1. Estimate the difference. Then use the standard subtraction algorithm to calculate the exact difference.

a. Estimate

_____

Th	H	T	O
7	0	6	7
− 2	4	6	1

b. Estimate

_____

TTh	Th	H	T	O
2	9	7	0	6
− 1	8	9	4	2

c. Estimate

_____

TTh	Th	H	T	O
3	0	4	5	7
− 1	8	3	2	9

2. Estimate each answer in your head. Then write equations to calculate the exact quotient.

a.
3,416 ÷ 2 = _____

b.
6,515 ÷ 5 = _____

c.
8,424 ÷ 6 = _____

Preparing for Module 9

Write a multiple for each factor.

a.
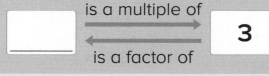

b.
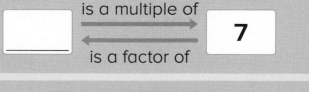

c.
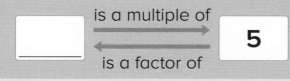

d.
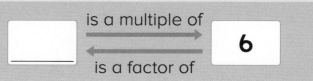

© ORIGO Education

Step In

Three friends share one pizza that is cut into eighths.
If they each eat one slice of pizza, how much pizza will be eaten?

How could you figure it out?

There are three people and they have $\frac{1}{8}$ of the pizza each. That is equivalent to $\frac{1}{8} + \frac{1}{8} + \frac{1}{8}$.

Another way to show this repeated addition is to use multiplication.

$3 \times \frac{1}{8}$

What multiplication equation could you write if each person had two slices?

Draw a picture to show your thinking.

Imagine there were two pizzas and the friends each eat three slices. What multiplication equation could you write to calculate the total?

When you multiply a fraction by a whole number, what do you notice?

Step Up

1. Each large shape is one whole. Complete each equation.

a.
 $3 \times \frac{2}{10} = \underline{\quad}$

b.
 $2 \times \frac{4}{12} = \underline{\quad}$

c.
 $4 \times \frac{1}{6} = \underline{\quad}$

d.
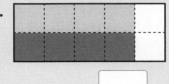 $2 \times \frac{4}{10} = \underline{\quad}$

e.
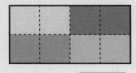 $4 \times \frac{2}{8} = \underline{\quad}$

2. Each large shape is one whole.
Color each shape to match the equation, then write the product.

a.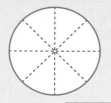

$$2 \times \frac{3}{8} = \underline{\hspace{1.5cm}}$$

b.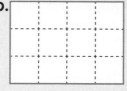

$$3 \times \frac{2}{12} = \underline{\hspace{1.5cm}}$$

c.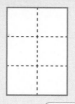

$$1 \times \frac{4}{6} = \underline{\hspace{1.5cm}}$$

d.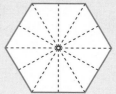

$$2 \times \frac{5}{12} = \underline{\hspace{1.5cm}}$$

3. Complete these equations.

a.
$$2 \times \frac{2}{6} = \underline{\hspace{1.5cm}}$$

b.
$$\underline{\hspace{1.5cm}} = 6 \times \frac{2}{10}$$

c.
$$3 \times \frac{4}{10} = \underline{\hspace{1.5cm}}$$

d.
$$\underline{\hspace{1.5cm}} = 4 \times \frac{5}{8}$$

4. Solve each problem. Show your thinking.

a. There were 2 glasses. Each was $\frac{5}{6}$ full of juice. How much juice was there in total?

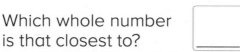 glasses of juice

Which whole number is that closest to? ___

b. Each straw was $\frac{2}{3}$ foot long. Nadia laid 5 of them end to end. What was the total length?

 feet

Which whole number is that closest to? ___

Step Ahead   Complete each equation.

a.
$$3 \times \frac{1}{8} \times 2 = \underline{\hspace{1.5cm}}$$

b.
$$4 \times \frac{2}{3} \times 7 = \underline{\hspace{1.5cm}}$$

c.
$$6 \times \frac{3}{5} \times 3 = \underline{\hspace{1.5cm}}$$

Common fractions: Exploring the multiplicative nature (number line model)

Step In

Archie needs 7 pieces of string that are each $\frac{3}{4}$ of a foot long. What is the total length of string he needs?

How does this number line show the problem?
Write the missing numerators in the fractions below the line.

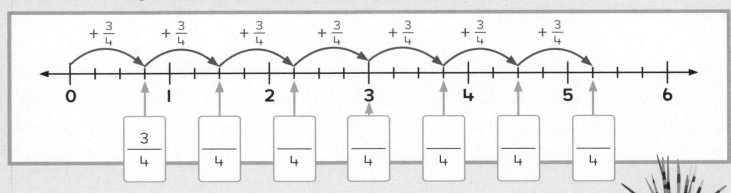

What multiplication equation could you write
to show the total length of string?

What do the jumps on the number line help you identify?
Look at the multiples of $\frac{3}{4}$ shown below the number line.
What do you notice about the numerators?

The jumps help me see
the fractions that
are multiples of $\frac{3}{4}$.

Step Up

1. The distance between each whole number is one whole.
   Draw jumps to show the equation. Then write the product.

a.

$4 \times \frac{5}{8} =$ ☐

b.

$5 \times \frac{4}{3} =$ ☐

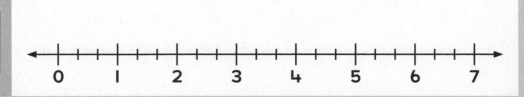

ORIGO Stepping Stones • Grade 4 • 8.10

2. Multiply each fraction by the number in the hexagon.
Write the products in the circles.

a.
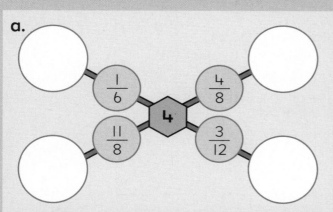

b.
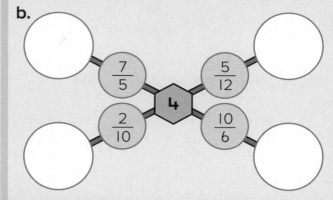

3. Write the first ten multiples of each fraction.

a. $\dfrac{3}{5}$

b. $\dfrac{5}{12}$

4. Circle the fractions in Question 3 that are between **1 and 2**.

5. Write a word problem to match this equation. Then write the product.

$$5 \times \dfrac{7}{8} =$$

Step Ahead   Write the missing numbers in each equation.

a. $\boxed{} \times \dfrac{2}{3} = \dfrac{8}{3}$

b. $5 \times \dfrac{\boxed{}}{\boxed{}} = \dfrac{5}{4}$

c. $\dfrac{18}{5} = \boxed{} \times \dfrac{3}{5}$

Computation Practice **Why is an old car like a baby?**

★ Complete the equations. Then write each letter above its matching difference at the bottom of the page. Some letters appear more than once.

$540 - 185 =$ ____ **v** $710 - 485 =$ ____ **w**

$450 - 265 =$ ____ **n** $850 - 575 =$ ____ **a**

$720 - 235 =$ ____ **o** $560 - 275 =$ ____ **i**

$330 - 275 =$ ____ **u** $950 - 475 =$ ____ **g**

$910 - 545 =$ ____ **h** $630 - 365 =$ ____ **s**

$550 - 295 =$ ____ **l** $420 - 185 =$ ____ **y**

$730 - 395 =$ ____ **r** $830 - 445 =$ ____ **e**

$620 - 455 =$ ____ **t**

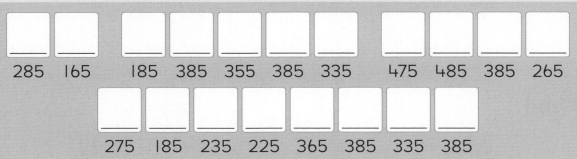

285 165   185 385 355 385 335   475 485 385 265

275 185 235 225 365 385 335 385

225 285 165 365 485 55 165   275   335 275 165 165 255 385

© ORIGO Education

ORIGO Stepping Stones · Grade 4 · 8.10

1. Use a protractor to measure and label the inside angles of the shape.

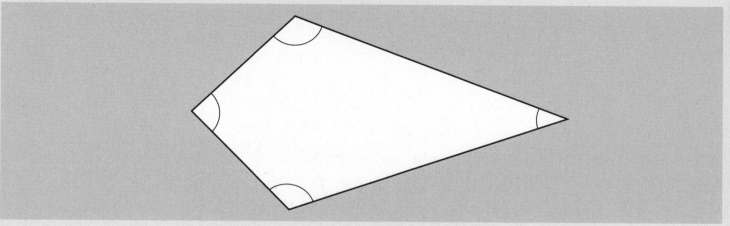

FROM 4.6.10

2. The distance between each whole number is one whole.
Draw jumps to show each equation. Then write the product.

FROM 4.8.10

a.

$3 \times \dfrac{4}{6} = $ ____

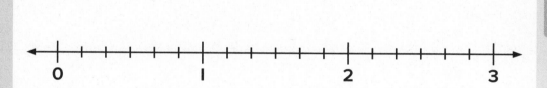

b.

$6 \times \dfrac{2}{3} = $ ____

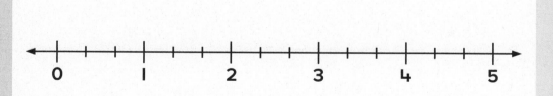

Preparing for Module 9

Write **less than**, **equal to**, or **more than** to describe the mass of each object compared to one pound.

a.

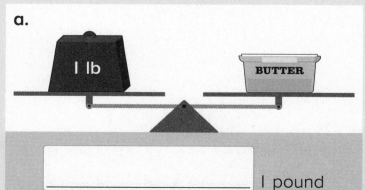

_____ 1 pound

b.

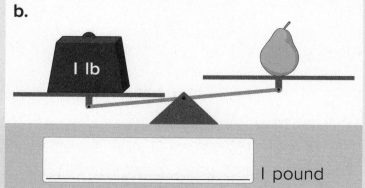

_____ 1 pound

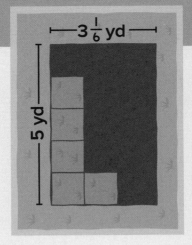

Step In   A groundskeeper is laying new turf in a rectangular section of the playing field.

The section measures 5 yards by $3\frac{1}{6}$ yards.
How many square yards of turf will be needed?

Alisa drew a picture like one she used to multiply whole numbers.

What do the numbers in her picture mean?

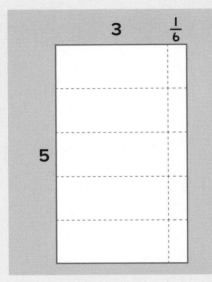

One dimension is three whole yards and $\frac{1}{6}$ of a yard. The other dimension is 5 yards.

Franco wrote this equation to represent the problem.

$$5 \times 3\frac{1}{6} = \boxed{}$$

Then he wrote this equation, which was easier to calculate.

$$(5 \times 3) + (5 \times \frac{1}{6}) = \boxed{}$$

How are the equations different? How are they the same?
What is the solution?

Look at Alisa's and Franco's methods.

How are they the same?
How are they different?

Which method do you prefer? Why?

Is there another way you could figure out the answer?

Step Up   Complete each calculation.

a.

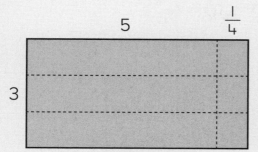

5    $\frac{1}{4}$

3

3 rows of 5 **and** 3 rows of $\frac{1}{4}$

$(3 \times \boxed{}) + (3 \times \boxed{\frac{}{}}) = \boxed{}$

b. 4 rows of 3 **and** 4 rows of $\frac{1}{6}$

$(4 \times \boxed{}) + (4 \times \boxed{\frac{}{}}) = \boxed{}$

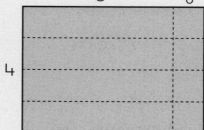

3    $\frac{1}{6}$

4

c.

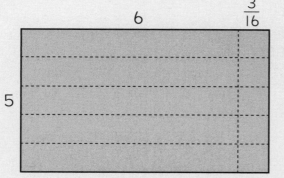

6    $\frac{3}{16}$

5

5 rows of 6 **and** 5 rows of $\frac{3}{16}$

$(5 \times \boxed{}) + (5 \times \boxed{\frac{}{}}) = \boxed{}$

d. 3 rows of 7 **and** 3 rows of $\frac{1}{8}$

$(3 \times \boxed{}) + (3 \times \boxed{\frac{}{}}) = \boxed{}$

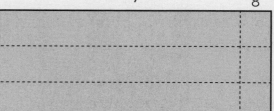

7    $\frac{1}{8}$

3

Step Ahead   Write the missing numbers on this trail.

$2\frac{1}{12}$ × 8 $\boxed{}$ $-9\frac{6}{12}$ $\boxed{}$ × 3 $\boxed{}$

Common fractions: Multiplying mixed numbers (with composing)

Victoria is painting a wall that is 7 feet high and $5\frac{1}{4}$ feet long.

What is the area of the wall? How could you figure it out?

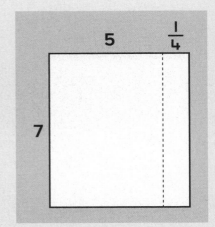

Jayden drew this picture to help him figure it out.
What numbers should you write below to match his picture?

(⬚ × ⬚) + (⬚ × ⬚)

What is the value of each partial product?

What do you need to do to the product of 7 and $\frac{1}{4}$ so the final answer makes sense?

What is the area of the wall?

Step Up

1. Write the partial products in each picture.

a.
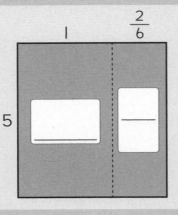

b.
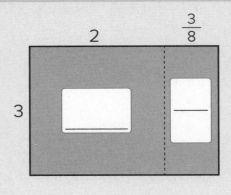

2. Write the missing numbers to calculate each product.

a. $5 \times 3\frac{1}{4}$

$$(5 \times \square) + (5 \times \frac{\square}{\quad})$$

$$\square + \frac{\square}{\quad} = \square$$

b. $3 \times 10\frac{5}{12}$

$$(3 \times \square) + (3 \times \frac{\square}{\quad})$$

$$\square + \frac{\square}{\quad} = \square$$

3. Solve each problem. Show your thinking.

a. Each bag of apples weighs $4\frac{1}{2}$ lb. How much do 6 bags weigh?

☐ lb

b. Each fence picket is $2\frac{1}{2}$ inches wide. What is the total width of 7 pickets?

☐ in

c. Each bottle holds $2\frac{1}{2}$ pints. How much do 8 bottles hold in total?

☐ pt

d. Each grape weighs $4\frac{3}{10}$ grams. What is the total mass of 7 grapes?

☐ g

Step Ahead   Complete these.

a.

☐ $\times 5\frac{3}{10} = 10\frac{6}{10}$

b.

$5 = $ ☐ $\times 1\frac{1}{4}$

c.

$15\frac{5}{8} = $ ☐ $\times 3\frac{1}{8}$

d.

$2 \times$ ☐ $= 1\frac{2}{8}$

Working Space

Think and Solve

What is the mystery number? _____

Clues

- It is less than 8 × 36.
- It is greater than 490 ÷ 2.
- It is a palindrome.
- It can be divided by 3.
- The sum of its digits is an even number.

> 636 and DAD are both **palindromes**, as they read the same from the left, and from the right.

Words at Work

Write in words how you know that these two equations will have the same answer.

$$\frac{2}{8} \times 4 = ?$$

$$\frac{2}{8} + \frac{2}{8} + \frac{2}{8} + \frac{2}{8} = ?$$

© ORIGO Education

Ongoing Practice

1. Look at the diagram. Use the clues to calculate the size of each angle. Do not use a protractor. Show your thinking.

Clues

- Angle **AOC** is 90°.
- Angle **AOD** is 120°.
- Angle **AOB** is 30°.
- Angle **AOE** is 180°.

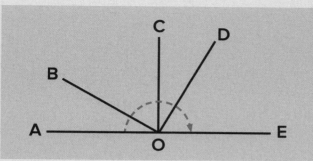

a.

Angle **BOC** is _____ °

b.

Angle **COD** is _____ °

c.

Angle **BOE** is _____ °

2. Write the missing numbers to calculate each product.

a.

$4 \times 2\frac{1}{3}$

$(4 \times \boxed{}) + (4 \times \dfrac{\boxed{}}{})$

$\boxed{} + \dfrac{\boxed{}}{} = \boxed{}$

b.

$5 \times 3\frac{2}{6}$

$(5 \times \boxed{}) + (5 \times \dfrac{\boxed{}}{})$

$\boxed{} + \dfrac{\boxed{}}{} = \boxed{}$

Preparing for Module 9

Write **more than**, **equal to**, or **less than** to describe the capacity of each container.

a.

16 pints

_____

3 quarts

b.

4 quarts

_____

1 gallon

c.

17 cups

_____

1 gallon

d.

1 gallon

_____

9 pints

FROM 4.6.12

FROM 4.8.11

© ORIGO Education

Step In

Callum and Bella each have an orange. Callum eats $\frac{1}{4}$ of his orange, and puts the rest in the refrigerator. Bella eats $\frac{3}{4}$ of her orange.

Who has more orange left over? How do you know?

Two friends compete in a running race.
Evan runs $\frac{3}{4}$ of the distance, and then walks the rest.
Bianca runs $\frac{3}{5}$ of the distance, and then walks the rest.

Who ran the greater distance? How can you tell?

This number line has been split into fourths and fifths.
Draw arrows to show how you could use it to compare the distance that each person ran.

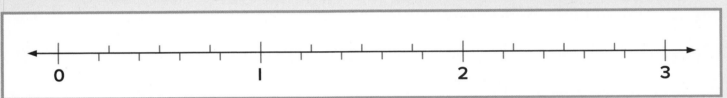

How could you use this number line to compare $\frac{11}{4}$ and $\frac{11}{5}$?

Step Up

1. On this number line the distance from 0 to 1 is one whole. Write **<** or **>** to complete each statement.

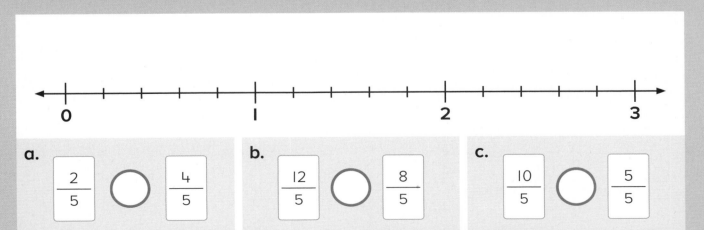

a. $\frac{2}{5}$ ◯ $\frac{4}{5}$

b. $\frac{12}{5}$ ◯ $\frac{8}{5}$

c. $\frac{10}{5}$ ◯ $\frac{5}{5}$

2. Write **<** or **>** to complete each statement. Use the number line to help your thinking.

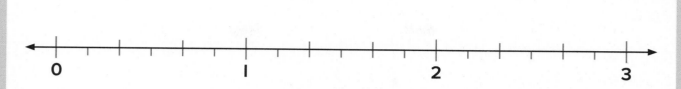

a.
$\frac{1}{3}$ ◯ $\frac{1}{6}$

b.
$\frac{3}{3}$ ◯ $\frac{3}{6}$

c.
$\frac{8}{6}$ ◯ $\frac{5}{6}$

d.
$\frac{8}{3}$ ◯ $\frac{4}{3}$

e.
$\frac{7}{6}$ ◯ $\frac{7}{3}$

f.
$\frac{9}{6}$ ◯ $\frac{9}{3}$

3. Use what you know about comparing fractions to complete each statement.

a.
$\frac{5}{8}$ ◯ $\frac{7}{8}$

b.
$\frac{10}{4}$ ◯ $\frac{10}{2}$

c.
$\frac{6}{5}$ ◯ $\frac{6}{3}$

d.
$\frac{12}{10}$ ◯ $\frac{9}{10}$

e.
$\frac{15}{3}$ ◯ $\frac{11}{3}$

f.
$\frac{7}{9}$ ◯ $\frac{7}{7}$

Step Ahead

a. Write a rule for comparing two fractions that have the same denominator.

b. Write a rule for comparing two fractions with the same numerator.

Step In   The top strip is one whole.

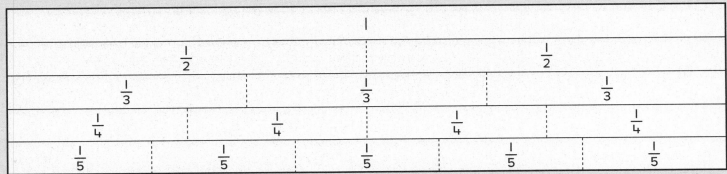

What do you notice about the number of parts in each strip?
What do you notice about the size of the parts in each strip?

Which fraction is greater?
How did you decide?

$$\frac{1}{2} \text{ or } \frac{1}{5}$$

Which fraction is greater?
What helps you figure it out?

$$\frac{1}{8} \text{ or } \frac{1}{10}$$

I think $\frac{1}{8}$ is greater than $\frac{1}{10}$. If you split a shape into 8 equal parts, each part would be bigger than if you split the shape into 10 equal parts.

Which fraction is greater?

$$\frac{1}{2} \text{ or } \frac{2}{5}$$

How could you use the fraction chart above to help you?
What is another way you could figure it out?

Step Up   I. Circle the fraction that is **greater** in each pair.
Use the fraction chart to help you.

a. $\frac{1}{5}$ or $\frac{1}{12}$

b. $\frac{3}{8}$ or $\frac{1}{2}$

c. $\frac{3}{5}$ or $\frac{9}{12}$

d. $\frac{4}{5}$ or $\frac{7}{8}$

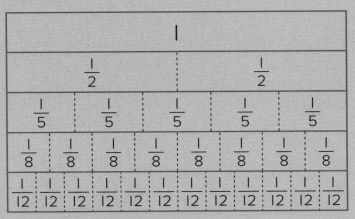

The top strip in this fraction chart shows two wholes.

1																							

The fraction chart shows:
- Top row split into two wholes, each labeled **1**
- $\frac{1}{2}$, $\frac{1}{2}$ | $\frac{1}{2}$, $\frac{1}{2}$
- $\frac{1}{3}$ ×3 | $\frac{1}{3}$ ×3
- $\frac{1}{4}$ ×4 | $\frac{1}{4}$ ×4
- $\frac{1}{6}$ ×6 | $\frac{1}{6}$ ×6
- $\frac{1}{12}$ ×12 | $\frac{1}{12}$ ×12

2. Write **=**, **<**, or **>** to make each statement true. Use the fraction chart to help you.

a. $\frac{3}{12}$ ◯ $\frac{1}{3}$

b. $\frac{5}{6}$ ◯ $\frac{1}{3}$

c. $\frac{10}{6}$ ◯ $\frac{10}{12}$

d. $\frac{4}{3}$ ◯ $\frac{8}{6}$

e. $\frac{6}{12}$ ◯ $\frac{12}{6}$

f. $\frac{3}{2}$ ◯ $\frac{2}{3}$

3. a. Write three fractions that are greater than $\frac{3}{4}$ but less than $\frac{14}{12}$. Use a variety of denominators.

____ ____ ____

b. Write three fractions that are greater than 1 but less than $\frac{7}{4}$. Use a variety of denominators.

____ ____ ____

Step Ahead

Choose fractions from below to complete the comparisons on the right. Use each fraction only once.

$\frac{3}{4}$ $\frac{8}{5}$ $\frac{3}{2}$ $\frac{9}{10}$ $\frac{7}{5}$ $\frac{13}{10}$

a. ____ is greater than ____

b. ____ is greater than ____

c. ____ is greater than ____

Computation Practice

Where can you always find a helping hand?

★ Complete the equations. Find each product in the grid below and cross out the letter above. Then write the remaining letters at the bottom of the page.

321 × 3 = _____

240 × 6 = _____

4 × 210 = _____

4 × 231 = _____

3 × 403 = _____

214 × 3 = _____

320 × 4 = _____

512 × 5 = _____

4 × 520 = _____

412 × 3 = _____

4 × 306 = _____

221 × 5 = _____

3 × 312 = _____

230 × 4 = _____

4 × 212 = _____

112 × 5 = _____

4 × 160 = _____

225 × 3 = _____

3 × 221 = _____

Write the letters in order from the ✳ to the bottom-right corner.

A	C	T	S	T	I	T	C	H
1,248	2,560	669	640	924	1,236	948	1,209	685
M	E	F	R	I	E	N	D	S
936	1,150	560	663	642	1,110	2,600	940	920
O	F	F	M	Y	O	W	N	U
875	896	963	2,080	2,580	1,436	1,280	675	820
R	E	A	C	H	R	M	U	M
1,444	848	860	1,440	1,224	2,460	1,105	840	880

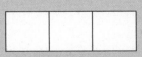

© ORIGO Education

Ongoing Practice

1. There are 12 inches in one foot and 3 feet in one yard.
Complete these to change yards to feet, and then to inches.

a. 4 yards

 [is equivalent to]

_____ ft

 [is equivalent to]

_____ in

b. 8 yards

 [is equivalent to]

_____ ft

 [is equivalent to]

_____ in

c. 7 yards

 [is equivalent to]

_____ ft

 [is equivalent to]

_____ in

2. On this number line the distance from 0 to 1 is one whole. Write **<** or **>** to complete each statement.

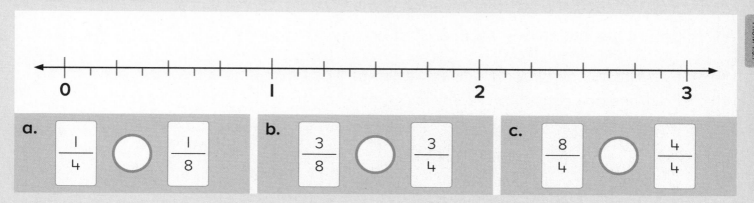

a. $\frac{1}{4}$ ◯ $\frac{1}{8}$

b. $\frac{3}{8}$ ◯ $\frac{3}{4}$

c. $\frac{8}{4}$ ◯ $\frac{4}{4}$

Preparing for Module 10

Each large shape is one whole.
Color the shapes to show the mixed number.

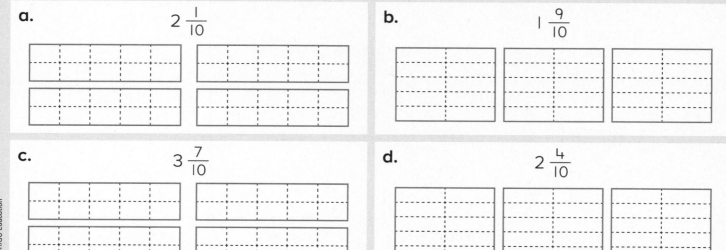

a. $2\frac{1}{10}$

b. $1\frac{9}{10}$

c. $3\frac{7}{10}$

d. $2\frac{4}{10}$

Step In

On this number line, the distance from 0 to 1 is one whole.

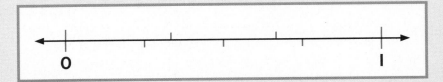

How has the number line been partitioned on the top? Name the fractions.
How has the number line been partitioned on the bottom? Name the fractions.

How could you use the number line to figure out if $\frac{2}{3}$ is greater than $\frac{3}{4}$?

On this number line, the distance from 0 to 1 is one whole.

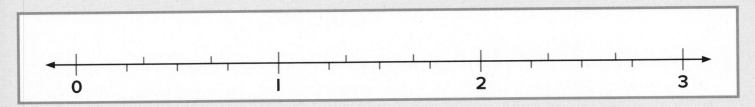

Which part of the line shows fractions that are greater than 1?

Which fractions are between 1 and 2? Which of those fractions is the greatest?
Which fractions are equivalent to 3?

Step Up

1. On each number line below, the distance from 0 to 1 is one whole. Circle the greater fraction in each pair. Use the number lines to help.

a. $\frac{2}{3}$ or $\frac{2}{4}$ b. $\frac{5}{4}$ or $\frac{3}{3}$ c. $\frac{13}{4}$ or $\frac{11}{3}$ d. $\frac{10}{3}$ or $\frac{12}{4}$

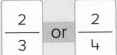 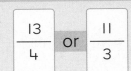 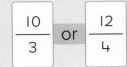

e. $\frac{3}{6}$ or $\frac{3}{4}$ f. $\frac{5}{4}$ or $\frac{7}{6}$ g. 2 or $\frac{9}{4}$ h. $\frac{11}{6}$ or $\frac{9}{4}$

 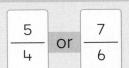 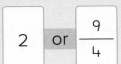 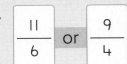

2. On each number line, the distance from 0 to 1 is one whole.
Write **<**, **>**, or **=** to make each statement true.

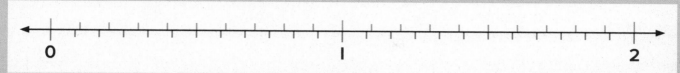

a. $\dfrac{6}{10}$ ◯ $\dfrac{9}{12}$ **b.** $\dfrac{13}{12}$ ◯ $\dfrac{11}{10}$ **c.** $\dfrac{15}{10}$ ◯ $\dfrac{2}{1}$ **d.** $\dfrac{12}{12}$ ◯ $\dfrac{9}{10}$

e. $\dfrac{10}{5}$ ◯ $\dfrac{16}{8}$ **f.** $\dfrac{13}{8}$ ◯ 2 **g.** $\dfrac{14}{5}$ ◯ $\dfrac{22}{8}$ **h.** $\dfrac{17}{8}$ ◯ $\dfrac{15}{5}$

3. Use the number lines in Questions 1 and 2 to help you write these fractions
in order from **least** to **greatest**.

a. $\dfrac{8}{6}$ $\dfrac{13}{6}$ $\dfrac{6}{4}$ $\dfrac{8}{4}$

___ ___ ___ ___

b. $\dfrac{5}{4}$ $\dfrac{8}{3}$ $\dfrac{13}{4}$ $\dfrac{2}{3}$

___ ___ ___ ___

c. $\dfrac{11}{12}$ $\dfrac{18}{10}$ $\dfrac{7}{12}$ $\dfrac{12}{10}$

___ ___ ___ ___

d. $\dfrac{11}{5}$ $\dfrac{18}{8}$ $\dfrac{4}{5}$ $\dfrac{3}{1}$

___ ___ ___ ___

e. $\dfrac{11}{4}$ $\dfrac{7}{4}$ $\dfrac{7}{6}$ $\dfrac{12}{6}$

___ ___ ___ ___

f. $\dfrac{2}{1}$ $\dfrac{24}{8}$ $\dfrac{12}{8}$ $\dfrac{5}{5}$

___ ___ ___ ___

Step Ahead

In each pair, circle the fraction that is closer to $\dfrac{1}{2}$. Use the number
lines on pages 326 and 327 to help you.

a. $\dfrac{4}{10}$ $\dfrac{5}{12}$ **b.** $\dfrac{2}{3}$ $\dfrac{3}{4}$ **c.** $\dfrac{3}{8}$ $\dfrac{2}{5}$ **d.** $\dfrac{1}{4}$ $\dfrac{2}{6}$

Step In

Kuma wanted to figure out an equivalent fraction for $\frac{5}{6}$.

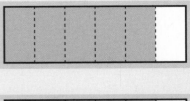

She drew this picture to help.

Kuma realized that if she drew another line horizontally, she would find an equivalent fraction.

She noticed that splitting the shape that way would double the value of the denominator.
What would happen to the numerator? Why?

Complete this diagram to show Kuma's thinking.

How did the total number of parts change?
How did the number of blue parts change?
Did the total area that was shaded change?

What do you notice about the denominators?

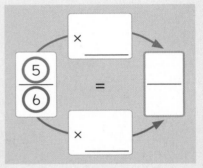

I see that 12 is a multiple of 6.

Step Up

1. In each shape, color a part to show the first fraction. Then draw more lines and complete the diagram to show an equivalent fraction.

a.

$$\frac{1}{4} = \frac{}{12}$$

b.

$$\frac{1}{3} = \frac{}{12}$$

c.

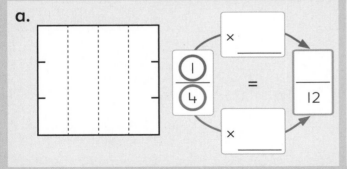

$$\frac{1}{2} = \frac{}{12}$$

d.

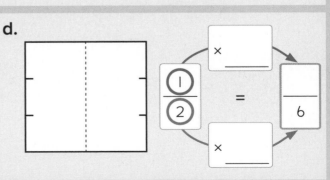

$$\frac{1}{2} = \frac{}{6}$$

2. Complete these to show equivalent fractions.

a.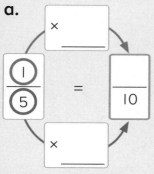

b.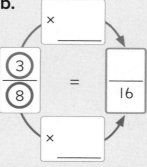

c.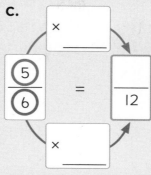

d.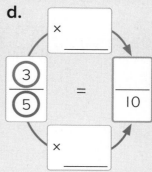

e.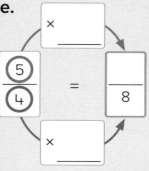

f.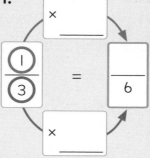

g.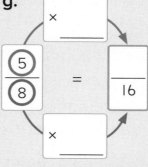

h.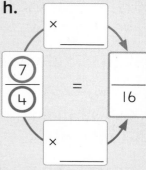

i.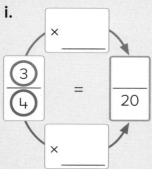

j.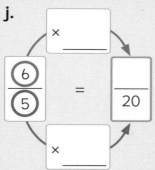

k.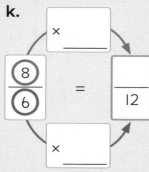

l.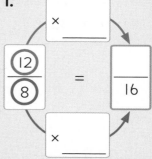

Step Ahead   Complete these to show equivalent fractions.

a.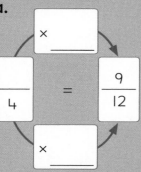

b.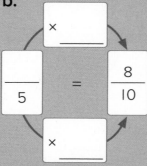

c.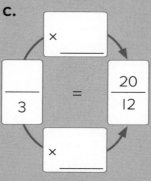

d.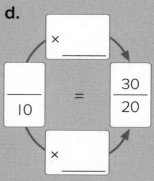

9.4　Maintaining concepts and skills

Think and Solve Read the clues. Figure out the five numbers and write them in order.

least　　　　　　　greatest

Clues

The least of the five numbers is 2.

The difference between the least number and the greatest number is 8.

The middle number is five more than the least number.

The sum of the five numbers is 30.

Words at Work

a. Look at this comparison. Is it true or false? Write in words how you decided.

$$\frac{9}{8} \quad < \quad \frac{13}{8}$$

b. Look at this comparison. Is it true or false? Write in words how you decided.

$$\frac{3}{16} \quad > \quad \frac{3}{7}$$

Ongoing Practice

1. There are 1,760 yards in one mile. Calculate the number of yards in each distance. Show your thinking.

a. 2 miles	b. 5 miles	c. 7 miles
_____ yd	_____ yd	_____ yd

2. Write **<**, **>**, or **=** to make each statement true. Show your thinking.

a. $\frac{2}{3}$ ◯ $\frac{3}{4}$

b. $\frac{3}{2}$ ◯ $\frac{4}{3}$

c. $\frac{5}{2}$ ◯ $\frac{10}{5}$

d. $\frac{8}{4}$ ◯ $\frac{6}{3}$

Preparing for Module 10

Complete the common fractions and mixed numbers.

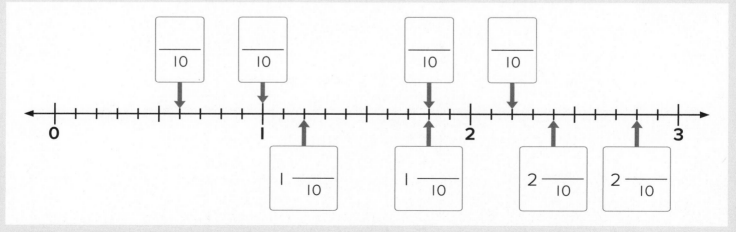

$\frac{}{10}$ $\frac{}{10}$ $\frac{}{10}$ $\frac{}{10}$

$1\frac{}{10}$ $1\frac{}{10}$ $2\frac{}{10}$ $2\frac{}{10}$

Step In

Henry and Anya each bought a blueberry pie on Saturday. On Sunday, they talked about how much pie their families had eaten.

Henry said his family ate $\frac{3}{5}$ of his pie.

Anya said that her family ate $\frac{8}{10}$ of her pie.

Whose family ate more pie? How could you figure it out?

I know that 10 is a multiple of 5, so I will change $\frac{3}{5}$ into tenths. If I double 5, I get 10. To make sure the fraction is equivalent, I need to double the numerator too. Then it is easy to compare the fractions.

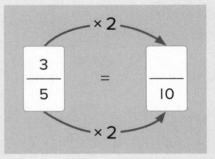

Hernando is making muffins. The recipe uses $\frac{3}{4}$ of a stick of butter.

There is $\frac{4}{8}$ of a stick of butter in the refrigerator.

Will Hernando have enough butter for the recipe? How could you figure it out?

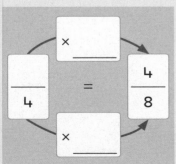

I know $\frac{4}{8}$ is equal to $\frac{1}{2}$ because 4 is half of 8. I also know that $\frac{3}{4}$ is more than $\frac{1}{2}$ because 2 is half of 4.

8 is a multiple of 4, so I would change $\frac{3}{4}$ into eighths then compare the fractions.

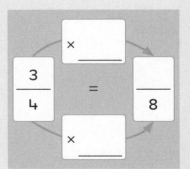

When I look at $\frac{4}{8}$, I can see the denominator is a multiple of 4. I might be able to change the fraction to fourths to help compare. If I change $\frac{4}{8}$ to fourths, what will the numerator become?

1. Change **one** fraction in each pair so that they have the same denominator. Then rewrite the fractions.

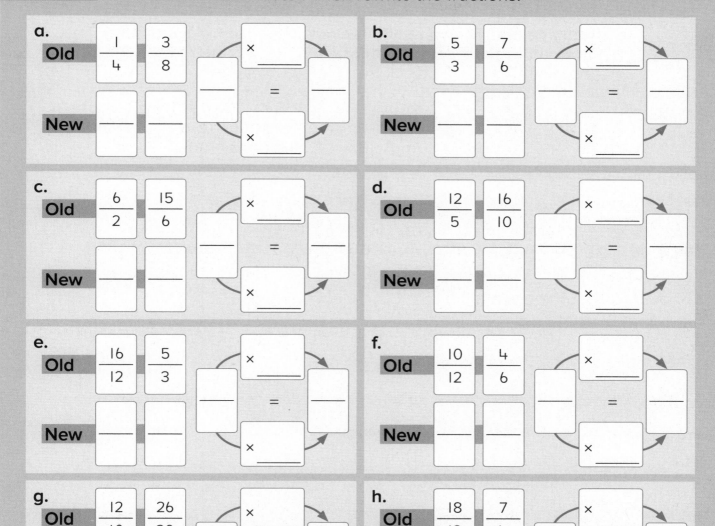

a.
Old $\dfrac{1}{4}$ $\dfrac{3}{8}$
New

b.
Old $\dfrac{5}{3}$ $\dfrac{7}{6}$
New

c.
Old $\dfrac{6}{2}$ $\dfrac{15}{6}$
New

d.
Old $\dfrac{12}{5}$ $\dfrac{16}{10}$
New

e.
Old $\dfrac{16}{12}$ $\dfrac{5}{3}$
New

f.
Old $\dfrac{10}{12}$ $\dfrac{4}{6}$
New

g.
Old $\dfrac{12}{10}$ $\dfrac{26}{20}$
New

h.
Old $\dfrac{18}{12}$ $\dfrac{7}{4}$
New

2. Circle the **greater** fraction in each pair of **new** fractions above.

Will a bolt that is $\dfrac{7}{16}$ of an inch wide fit into a hole that is $\dfrac{3}{8}$ of an inch wide? Why?

Step In

Anna compares two muffin recipes. One uses $\frac{2}{3}$ cup of flour. The other recipe uses $\frac{3}{4}$ cup of flour.

Which recipe uses more flour?
How can you figure it out?

Hmmm... this is a little tricky. Neither denominator is a multiple of the other one.

What could you do to both denominators to make equivalent fractions?

You could find a multiple that is the same for each denominator.

How could you figure out what multiple they have in common?

Marvin figured it out by listing all the multiples of 3 that he knew.
He then started listing the multiples of 4.

| 3 | 6 | 9 | 12 | 15 | 18 | 21 | 24 | 27 | 30 |

| 4 | 8 | 12 |

Circle the multiple that is common to both denominators.

Complete each diagram to show equivalent fractions for $\frac{2}{3}$ and $\frac{3}{4}$.

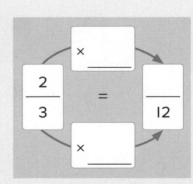

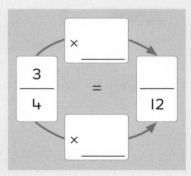

Which fraction is greater?

Step Up

1. Identify whether you have to change **one** denominator or **both** denominators to compare the fractions. Color the ◯ beside the statement that is correct.

a.
  $\frac{2}{4}$ $\frac{5}{8}$
  ◯ I need to change one.
  ◯ I need to change both.

b.
  $\frac{2}{5}$ $\frac{3}{8}$
  ◯ I need to change one.
  ◯ I need to change both.

c.
  $\frac{2}{3}$ $\frac{4}{5}$
  ◯ I need to change one.
  ◯ I need to change both.

2. Circle the common multiples.

a.

Multiples of 3	3	6	9	12	15	18	21	24	27	30
Multiples of 5	5	10	15	20	25	30	35	40	45	50

b.

Multiples of 4	4	8	12	16	20	24	28	32	36	40
Multiples of 6	6	12	18	24	30	36	42	48	54	60

3. For each pair of fractions, complete the diagram to show equivalent fractions that have a common denominator. Then complete the statement. Use the common multiples in Question 2 to help you.

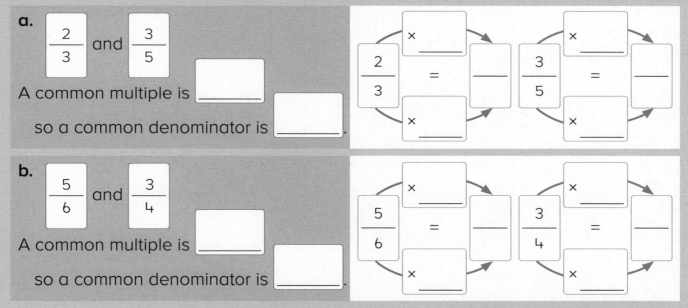

a. $\frac{2}{3}$ and $\frac{3}{5}$

A common multiple is _____

so a common denominator is _____.

b. $\frac{5}{6}$ and $\frac{3}{4}$

A common multiple is _____

so a common denominator is _____.

Step Ahead

In some problems, a common denominator can be found by using division and looking for common factors.

a. Rewrite $\frac{12}{18}$ and $\frac{10}{12}$ as fractions with a common denominator of 6.

b. Which fraction is greater? _____

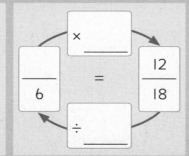
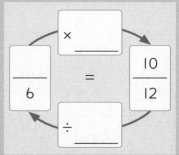

Computation Practice

★ Use a ruler to draw a straight line from each division card to the correct quotient. The line will pass through a letter. Write the letter above its matching quotient at the bottom of the page to show a nature fact. Some letters appear more than once.

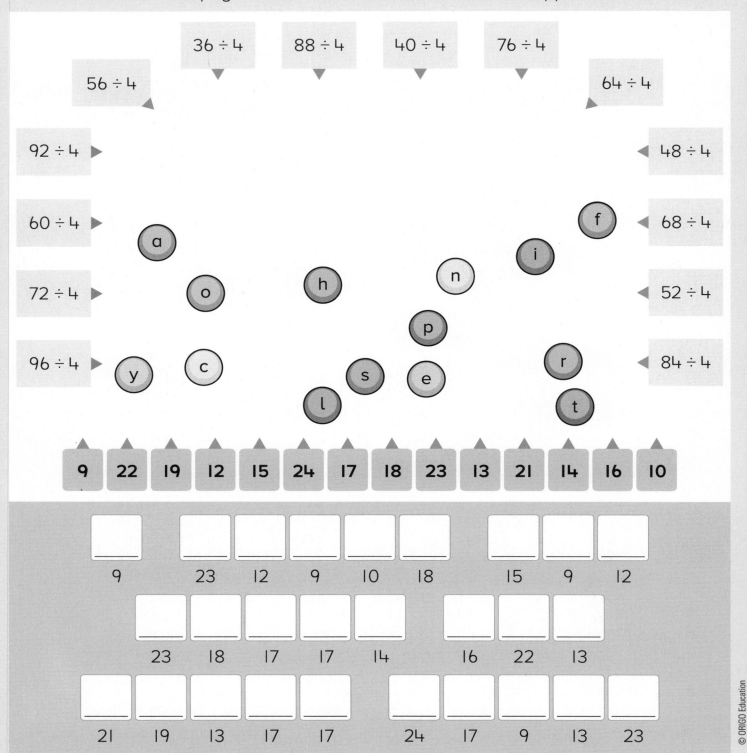

© ORIGO Education

Ongoing Practice

I. Calculate the area of each rectangle. Show your thinking.

a.

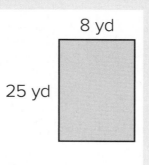

25 yd

8 yd

Area _____ yd²

b.

24 yd

5 yd

Area _____ yd²

2. On this number line, the distance from 0 to I is one whole. In each pair, circle the fraction that is **greater**. Use the number line to help.

a. $\dfrac{2}{5}$ or $\dfrac{3}{4}$ **b.** $\dfrac{6}{4}$ or $\dfrac{7}{5}$ **c.** $\dfrac{9}{4}$ or $\dfrac{11}{5}$ **d.** $\dfrac{15}{4}$ or $\dfrac{19}{5}$

0   1   2   3   4

e. $\dfrac{2}{4}$ or $\dfrac{3}{5}$ **f.** $\dfrac{9}{5}$ or $\dfrac{8}{4}$ **g.** $\dfrac{10}{4}$ or $\dfrac{12}{5}$ **h.** $\dfrac{17}{5}$ or $\dfrac{14}{4}$

Preparing for Module 10

Write the missing numbers to make each statement true. Use the place-value chart to help your thinking.

a. 10 is _____ times greater than I.

b. 10,000 is _____ times greater than 100.

c. 100,000 is _____ times greater than 1,000.

d. 10,000 is _____ times greater than 10.

e. _____ is 10 times greater than 10.

f. 100,000 is 10 times greater than _____.

Thousands			Ones		
H	T	O	H	T	O

×10   ×10   ×10   ×10   ×10

Step In Look at these multiples of 5 and 8.

| Multiples of 5: | 5 | 10 | 15 | 20 | 25 | 30 | 35 | 40 | 45 | 50 |
| Multiples of 8: | 8 | 16 | 24 | 32 | 40 | 48 | 56 | 64 | 72 | 80 |

What is a common multiple of 5 and 8 that is listed above? _____

Now multiply 5 × 8. What do you notice?

Look at these multiples of 3 and 5.

| Multiples of 3: | 3 | 6 | 9 | 12 | 15 | 18 | 21 | 24 | 27 | 30 |
| Multiples of 5: | 5 | 10 | 15 | 20 | 25 | 30 | 35 | 40 | 45 | 50 |

Which are the common multiples? _____

Now multiply 3 × 5. What do you notice?

How could you use this to help you write common denominators?

When I multiply the denominators together, I get a multiple of each denominator. That is much faster than having to list all the multiples of each denominator.

What is a common multiple of 3 and 8? _____

Use what you know to rewrite $\frac{2}{3}$ and $\frac{6}{8}$ so they have a common denominator.

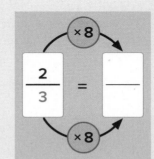

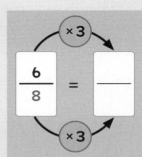

Step Up 1. Write a common multiple of each pair of numbers.

a.
2 and 8 _____

b.
10 and 4 _____

c.
5 and 2 _____

d.
5 and 6 _____

2. For each pair of fractions, complete the diagram to show equivalent fractions that have a common denominator. Then complete the sentence.

a. $\dfrac{3}{4}$ **and** $\dfrac{5}{6}$

A common multiple is _____

so a common denominator is _____ .

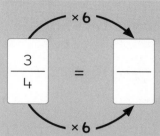

$$\dfrac{3}{4} = \dfrac{}{}$$

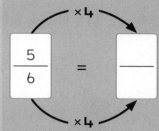

$$\dfrac{5}{6} = \dfrac{}{}$$

b. $\dfrac{9}{4}$ **and** $\dfrac{7}{5}$

A common multiple is _____

so a common denominator is _____ .

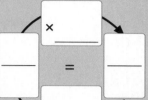

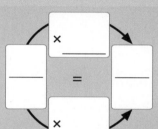

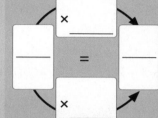

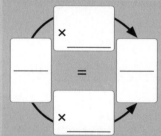

c. $\dfrac{3}{5}$ **and** $\dfrac{9}{12}$

A common multiple is _____

so a common denominator is _____ .

3. Write **<**, **>**, or **=** to make each statement true. Show your thinking.

a. $\dfrac{7}{5} \bigcirc \dfrac{3}{2}$

b. $\dfrac{8}{3} \bigcirc \dfrac{5}{2}$

Step Ahead

Which fraction is the greatest? Show your thinking.

$\dfrac{7}{3}$ or $\dfrac{5}{2}$ or $\dfrac{12}{5}$ _____

© ORIGO Education

Step In   Look at these two fractions.

$\frac{2}{3}$ $\frac{4}{5}$

What strategy would you use to decide which is greater?

I would compare them to the benchmark 1.
They are both less than 1.
$\frac{2}{3}$ is $\frac{1}{3}$ away from 1 but $\frac{4}{5}$ is only $\frac{1}{5}$ away from 1.

Chloe looks for a **common denominator**.

What is a common multiple of 3 and 5?

Complete the diagram.

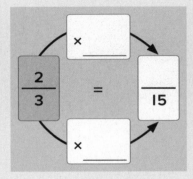

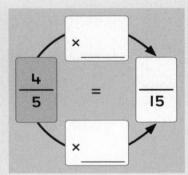

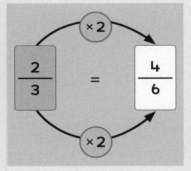

I could also find a common numerator.
4 is a multiple of 2, so I would only have
to change one numerator.

The fractions $\frac{4}{6}$ and $\frac{4}{5}$ are compared when you find
a common numerator.

How could this strategy be used to help make comparisons?

Step Up   1. Write **<** or **>** to make each statement true. Then explain the thinking
you used to make each comparison.

a. $\frac{6}{7}$ ◯ $\frac{8}{9}$ _____

b. $\frac{4}{6}$ ◯ $\frac{3}{8}$ _____

2. Write **<** or **>** to make each statement true. Write or show your thinking.

a. $\dfrac{1}{5}$ ◯ $\dfrac{1}{4}$

b. $\dfrac{3}{4}$ ◯ $\dfrac{5}{8}$

c. $\dfrac{5}{6}$ ◯ $\dfrac{9}{10}$

d. $\dfrac{3}{8}$ ◯ $\dfrac{6}{10}$

e. $\dfrac{6}{5}$ ◯ $\dfrac{3}{2}$

f. $\dfrac{6}{4}$ ◯ $\dfrac{9}{8}$

Step Ahead   Write these fractions in order from **least** to **greatest**.

$\dfrac{5}{2}$ $\dfrac{7}{3}$ $\dfrac{13}{5}$ ▢ ▢ ▢

Write or show your thinking.

Think and Solve What are the numbers? Show your thinking.

The product of three different numbers is 60.

The sum of the numbers is 17.

Words at Work

Write in words two different ways to find a common denominator to compare the fractions $\frac{2}{6}$ and $\frac{4}{9}$. Then write which fraction is greater.

Ongoing Practice

1. Imagine you wanted to lay turf in this barnyard.
   Calculate the area. Show your thinking.

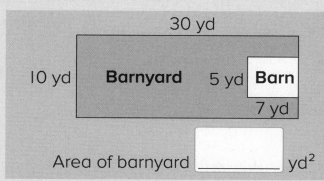

Area of barnyard _____ yd² .

2. Change **one** fraction in each pair so they have the same denominator.
   Then rewrite the fractions.

a.
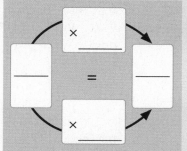
Old $\frac{2}{3}$ $\frac{2}{6}$
New

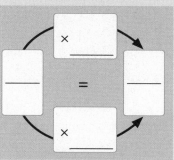

b.
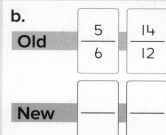
Old $\frac{5}{6}$ $\frac{14}{12}$
New

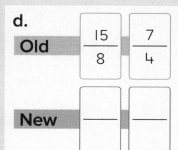

c.
Old $\frac{8}{3}$ $\frac{25}{12}$
New

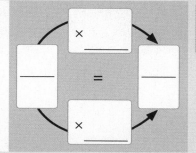

d.
Old $\frac{15}{8}$ $\frac{7}{4}$
New

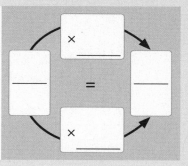

Preparing for Module 10   Write each number in expanded form.

a. 601,248 _____

b. 517,163 _____

FROM 4.3.9

FROM 4.9.5

Step In   Do you think an apple weighs more or less than one pound?

What are some other items that weigh less than one pound?

A granola bar would weigh less than one pound.

What unit of measure is used to describe something that weighs less than one pound?

I have seen **oz** written on jars and packets of food.

There are 16 ounces in one pound. A short way to write pound is **lb**. A short way to write ounce is **oz**. Ounce comes from the old Italian word **onza**.

Step Up   1. Three baseballs weigh about one pound in total. Think about the **real mass** of each item below. Then write the name of each item in the matching column of the table.

| stapler | cellphone | laptop | baseball bat |
| banana | eraser | pencil | bowling ball |

Weighs Less Than One Pound	Weighs More Than One Pound

2. Circle the bag of items that weighs **more than 1 lb** in total.

3. Circle the bag of items that weighs **more than 2 lb** in total.

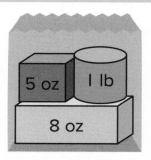  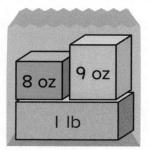

4. Solve each problem. Show your thinking.

a. Bag A weighs 2 lb. Bag B weighs 3 oz less than Bag A. How much does Bag B weigh?

_____ oz

b. A large bag of rice weighs 2 lb. A small bag of rice weighs 8 oz. How many times heavier is the large bag than the small bag?

_____

Step Ahead   Look at each balance picture. Circle the picture that is true.

Mass: Exploring the relationship between pounds and ounces

Step In

How could you calculate the difference in mass between these two bags?

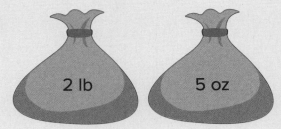

2 lb   5 oz

I would change the pounds into ounces to find the difference. There are 16 oz in 1 lb, so that is 32 - 5.

Complete these statements.

I pound = _____ ounces $\frac{1}{2}$ pound = _____ ounces $\frac{1}{4}$ pound = _____ ounces

How could you calculate the difference in mass between these two boxes?

What equation would you write?

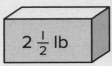 $2\frac{1}{2}$ lb   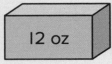 12 oz

Step Up

1. Calculate the difference in mass for each pair of bags. Show your thinking.

a.

3 lb   9 oz

_____ oz

b.

12 oz   5 lb

_____ oz

2. Calculate the difference in mass. Show your thinking.

a.

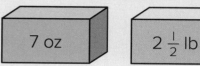

_____ oz

b.

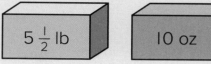

_____ oz

3. Solve each problem. Show your thinking.

a. Six muffins together weigh 4 oz less than a cake that weighs $1\frac{1}{2}$ lb. How much do the muffins weigh together?

_____ oz

b. $2\frac{1}{2}$ lb of flour is poured equally into 4 containers. How much flour is in each container?

_____ oz

Step Ahead Write the missing mass in each balance picture.

a.

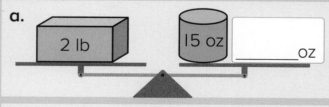

_____ oz

b.

_____ oz

c.

_____ oz

d.

_____ oz

Computation Practice   What are red velvet swords, firemouths, and tiger barbs?

★ Use a ruler to draw a line to the correct answer. The line will pass through a number and a letter. Write each letter above its matching number at the bottom of the page.

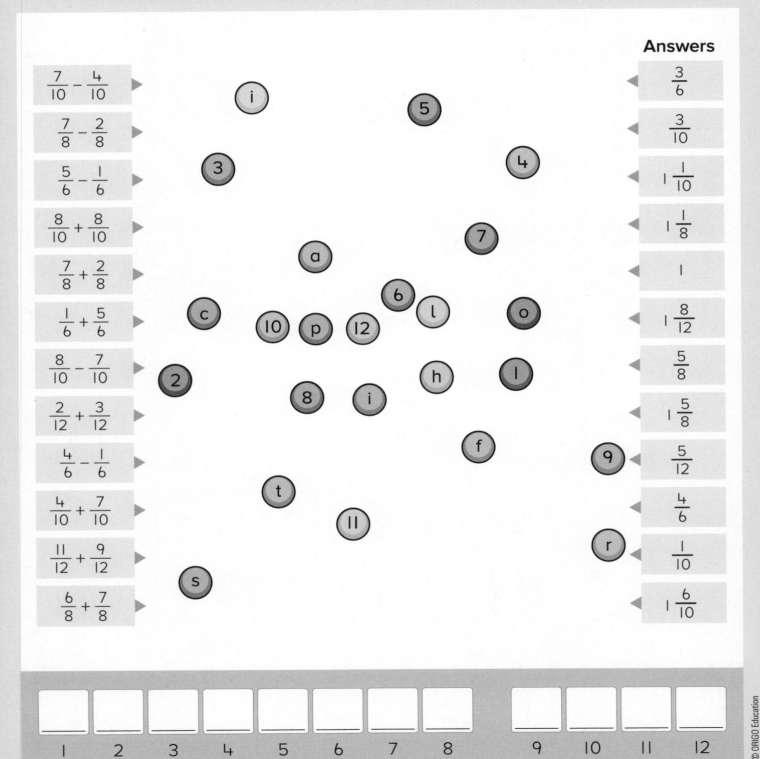

Answers

$\frac{7}{10} - \frac{4}{10}$

$\frac{7}{8} - \frac{2}{8}$

$\frac{5}{6} - \frac{1}{6}$

$\frac{8}{10} + \frac{8}{10}$

$\frac{7}{8} + \frac{2}{8}$

$\frac{1}{6} + \frac{5}{6}$

$\frac{8}{10} - \frac{7}{10}$

$\frac{2}{12} + \frac{3}{12}$

$\frac{4}{6} - \frac{1}{6}$

$\frac{4}{10} + \frac{7}{10}$

$\frac{11}{12} + \frac{9}{12}$

$\frac{6}{8} + \frac{7}{8}$

$\frac{3}{6}$

$\frac{3}{10}$

$1\frac{1}{10}$

$1\frac{1}{8}$

1

$1\frac{8}{12}$

$\frac{5}{8}$

$1\frac{5}{8}$

$\frac{5}{12}$

$\frac{4}{6}$

$\frac{1}{10}$

$1\frac{6}{10}$

1	2	3	4	5	6	7	8	9	10	11	12

Ongoing Practice

1. Complete these to calculate the perimeter of each rectangle.

a.

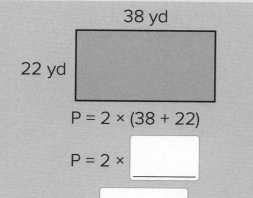

38 yd

22 yd

$P = 2 \times (38 + 22)$

$P = 2 \times$ ☐_____

$P =$ ☐_____ yd

b.

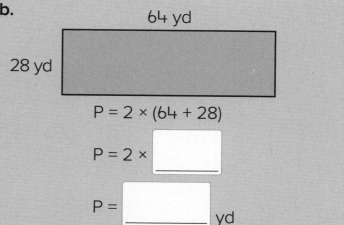

64 yd

28 yd

$P = 2 \times (64 + 28)$

$P = 2 \times$ ☐_____

$P =$ ☐_____ yd

2. Circle the bag of items that weighs 2 lb in total.

4 oz

1 lb   9 oz

7 oz

8 oz   13 oz

1 lb

6 oz   10 oz

Preparing for Module 10

Count on from one mixed number to calculate the total. Draw jumps on the number line to show your thinking.

a.

$1\frac{3}{5} + 1\frac{3}{5} =$ ☐

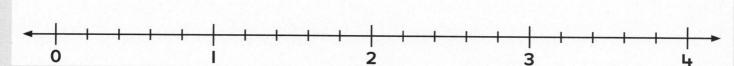

0   1   2   3   4

b.

$1\frac{3}{4} + 2\frac{3}{4} =$ ☐

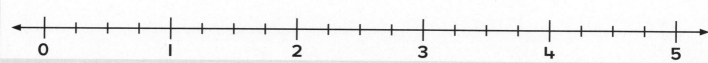

0   1   2   3   4   5

Step In   This table shows the number of containers that are required to make one gallon.

What do you notice?

Size of Container	Number of Containers
Quart	
Pint	
Cup	

I can see a doubling pattern. I quart is equal to 2 pints or 4 cups.

Complete this statement.

I gallon = _____ quarts = _____ pints = _____ cups

What is a unit of capacity that is less than one cup?

A fluid ounce is less than a cup.

There are 8 fluid ounces in one cup. A short way to write fluid ounce is fl oz.

Step Up   1. Calculate the number of fluid ounces in each of these units.

I pint = _____ fl oz

I quart = _____ fl oz

I gallon = _____ fl oz

Working Space

© ORIGO Education

2. Solve each problem. Show your thinking.

a. There is half a gallon of water in a sink. Another quart of water is poured into the sink. How much water is in the sink now?

_____ qt

b. Helen buys 2 1 qt bottles of juice. Manuel buys 10 bottles of juice that each holds 8 fl oz. Who buys the greater amount of juice?

_____

c. Hannah opens a one-gallon bottle of milk. She fills 4 glasses with milk. Each glass holds 16 fl oz. How much milk is left in the bottle?

_____ fl oz

d. There are 150 fl oz in a bottle of detergent. Each load of laundry uses 2 fl oz. How much detergent is left after 3 loads?

_____ fl oz

Step Ahead   Write numbers to make these balance pictures true.

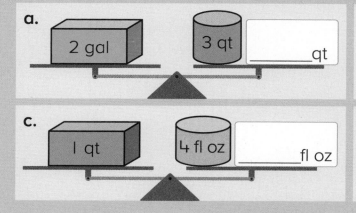

a. 2 gal = 3 qt _____ qt

c. 1 qt = 4 fl oz _____ fl oz

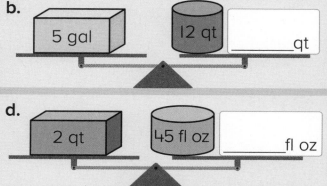

b. 5 gal = 12 qt _____ qt

d. 2 qt = 45 fl oz _____ fl oz

Capacity/mass: Solving word problems involving customary units

What can you see in this picture?

Imagine each small glass holds 8 fl oz.

How many small glasses could you fill from one bottle of water?
How do you know?

How many glasses could you fill with grape juice?

| 1 lb = 16 oz |
| 1 qt = 32 fl oz |
| 1 gal = 128 fl oz |

Each muffin weighs about 7 oz. What is the total mass of the muffins?

Is the total mass greater or less than 2 lb? How do you know?

Step Up

1. Solve each problem. Show your thinking.

a. Bottled water is sold in packs of 6. Each small bottle holds 17 fl oz. How much water will be in 2 packs?	b. Mika buys 1 lb of cheese. He cuts the cheese into 4 equal pieces then eats one piece. How much cheese is left?
_____ fl oz	_____ oz

2. Solve each problem. Remember to use the correct unit of measurement. Show your thinking.

a. Each bottle of water holds 1 qt. Each can holds 12 fl oz. How much water is in $1\frac{1}{2}$ bottles and 3 cans?

b. Deon buys 3 16 oz boxes of raisins. He shares the raisins equally among 4 bowls. What is the mass of raisins in each bowl?

c. Two 1 gallon bottles of water are poured equally into 8 pitchers. How many fluid ounces of water is in each pitcher?

d. Hunter has a 1 gal milk jug. Each drinking glass holds 8 fl oz. How many times greater is the capacity of the jug than a glass?

Step Ahead   Write numbers to complete the story. Make sure it make sense.

Andrea buys a carton of juice. The carton holds _____ fluid ounces. She fills

_____ glasses with juice from the carton. Each glass holds _____ fluid ounces.

There are _____ fl oz left in the carton.

Think and Solve

Look at this grid.

Change the position of two numbers in the grid so the sum of every row and column is a multiple of 10.

Write numbers in the blank grid to show the new positions.

14	27	7	13
37	11	18	4
3	12	8	17
16	1	6	26

Words at Work

Describe the relationships between gallons, quarts, pints, cups, and fluid ounces.

Ongoing Practice

1. Calculate the perimeter of each rectangle. Show your thinking.

a.

32 yd

28 yd

Perimeter _____ yd

b.

55 yd

47 yd

Perimeter _____ yd

2. Solve each problem. Show your thinking.

a. Carter buys 3 lb of nuts. He shares them equally between 4 bowls. How many ounces does he put in each bowl?

_____ oz

b. Monique packed 2 lb of apples, $1\frac{1}{2}$ lb of bananas, and 12 oz of berries into a bag. What is the total mass of the bag in ounces?

_____ oz

Preparing for Module 10

Solve each problem. Write the total as a mixed number. Draw a picture to show your thinking.

a. Ramon bought $\frac{3}{4}$ lb of potatoes and $\frac{2}{4}$ lb of onions. What was the total mass?

_____ lb

b. A recipe needs $\frac{3}{8}$ qt of juice and $\frac{6}{8}$ qt of water. How much liquid is used?

_____ qt

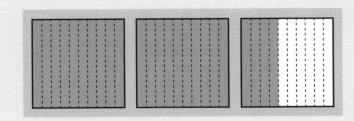

Step In   Look at this picture.

Each square is one whole.
What amount is shaded?

What are the different ways you can write this number without using words?

When fractions have a denominator that is a power of 10, they can easily be written in a place-value chart. Powers of 10 include numbers such as 10, 100, 1,000, and so on.

A number such as $2\frac{4}{10}$ can be written like this.

The red dot is called a **decimal point**. The decimal point is a mark that identifies the ones place.

Ones	tenths
2 .	4

Where have you seen numbers written with a decimal point?

I've seen a decimal point used for prices like $3.99.

Sometimes packets of food use a decimal point for masses, like 3.5 lb.

Look at the expanders below.

How would you say the number that each expander shows?

A **decimal fraction** is a fraction with no denominator visible. The denominator is determined by the number of places to the right of the decimal point.

How do these numbers relate to mixed numbers and common fractions?

Why do you need to show the decimal point when the expander is completely closed?

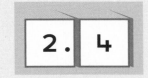

Step Up

1. Each square is one whole. Read the fraction name and shade the squares to match. Write the decimal fraction on the open expander.

a. two and five-tenths

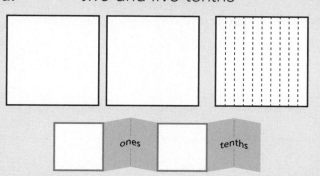

b. one and seven-tenths

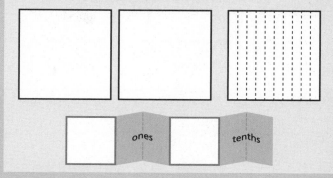

c. one and three-tenths

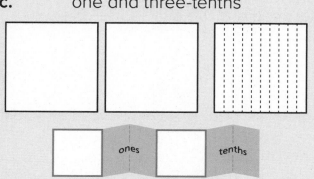

d. two and six-tenths

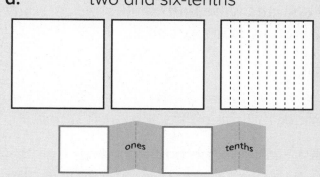

2. Read the fraction name. Write the amount as a common fraction or mixed number. Then write the matching decimal fraction on the expander.

a. four and two-tenths

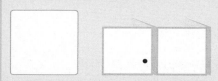

b. sixty-three tenths

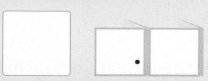

c. five and eight-tenths

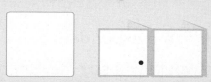

Step Ahead   Read the clues. Write a number on the expander to match.

a. I am greater than three and less than four. The digit in my tenths place is less than the digit in my ones place.

b. I am less than five and greater than one. The digit in my ones place is twice the value of the digit in my tenths place.

Step In

Look at the number line below. The distance between each whole number is one whole.

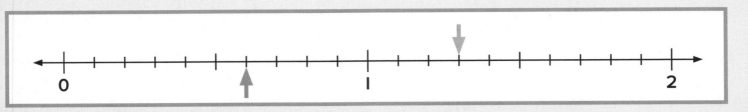

What fraction is the top arrow pointing to? How do you know?

Write it as a common fraction and as a mixed number.

$$\frac{}{10}$$ $$\frac{}{10}$$

Complete these expanders to show the same fraction.

☐ ones   ☐ tenths   ☐ . ☐

What fraction is the bottom arrow pointing to?
Can you write it as a common fraction and as a mixed number? Why?
What would it look like on an expander?

Think about how you compare 267 and 305 to figure out which number is greater.
Which place do you look at first?

ⓘ A zero is used in the ones place when the amount is less than one. This makes it easy to quickly see whether it is a whole number or a fraction.

Think about the fractions indicated by the arrows on the number line above.
What do they look like as decimal fractions?
Which is greater?
How can you tell by looking at their places?

Step Up

1. On this number line, the distance between each whole number is one whole. Write the decimal fraction that is shown by each arrow.

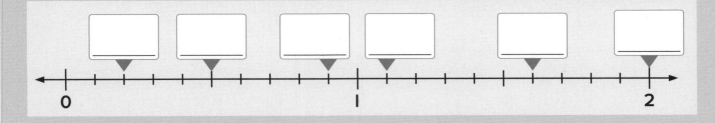

Use the masses of these fruit and vegetables to answer the questions on this page.

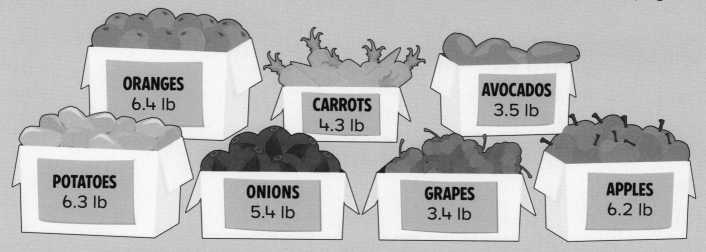

ORANGES
6.4 lb

CARROTS
4.3 lb

AVOCADOS
3.5 lb

POTATOES
6.3 lb

ONIONS
5.4 lb

GRAPES
3.4 lb

APPLES
6.2 lb

2. In each pair below, circle the box of fruit or vegetables that is **heavier**.

a. apples   **or**   onions

b. oranges   **or**   potatoes

c. apples   **or**   avocados

d. carrots   **or**   grapes

3. Write the masses. Then write **<** or **>** to make the statement true.

a. avocados   potatoes

_____ lb ◯ _____ lb

b. onions   grapes

_____ lb ◯ _____ lb

c. oranges   apples

_____ lb ◯ _____ lb

d. avocados   onions

_____ lb ◯ _____ lb

Step Ahead

Write the masses of the fruit and vegetables in order from **least** to **greatest**. Then draw a line to connect each mass to its approximate position on the number line.

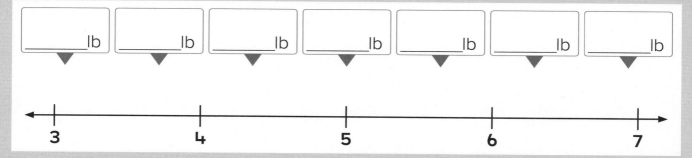

_____ lb   _____ lb   _____ lb   _____ lb   _____ lb   _____ lb   _____ lb

3   4   5   6   7

Computation Practice   What question can you never say "yes" to?

⭐ Use a ruler to draw a straight line to the correct product. The line will pass through a letter. Write each letter below its matching product.

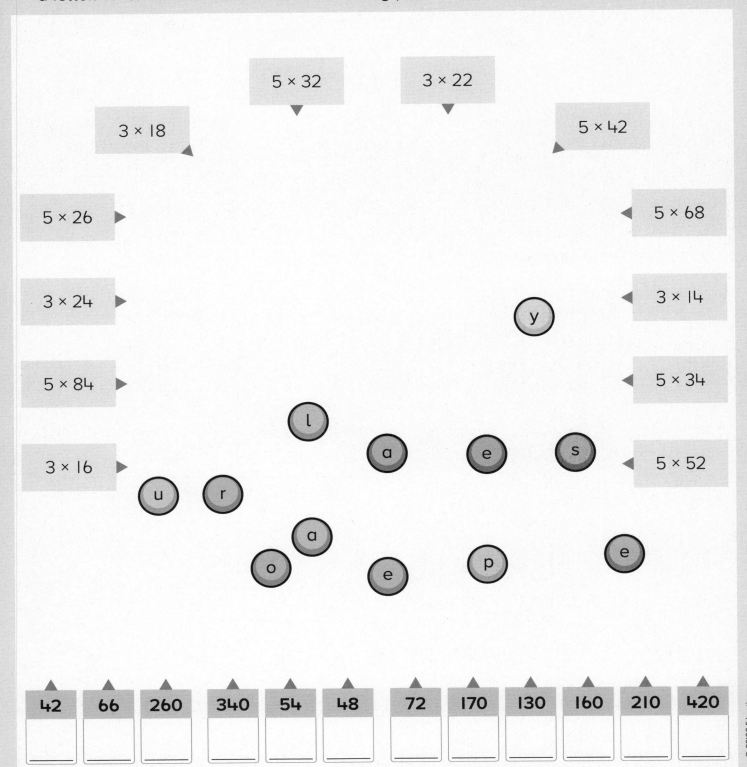

42	66	260	340	54	48	72	170	130	160	210	420

Ongoing Practice

1. Complete each of these.

a. $3\frac{6}{10}$ kg

is equivalent to

_____ g

b. 12 kg

is equivalent to

_____ g

c. $5\frac{1}{4}$ kg

is equivalent to

_____ g

d. $4\frac{1}{2}$ kg

is equivalent to

_____ g

e. 21 kg

is equivalent to

_____ g

f. $1\frac{8}{10}$ kg

is equivalent to

_____ g

2. Each square is one whole. Read the fraction name and shade the squares to match. Write the decimal fraction on the open expander.

a. one and six-tenths

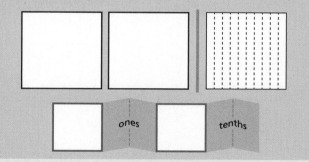

b. two and eight-tenths

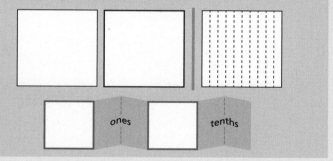

c. three and one-tenth

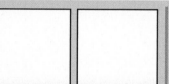

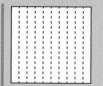

Preparing for Module 11

Calculate each partial product. Then write the total.

6 | 30 | 5

6 × _____ = _____

6 × _____ = _____

Total _____

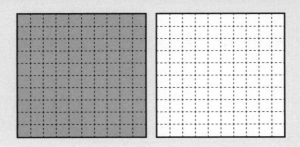

Step In Each large square represents one whole.

How many columns are in the shaded square?

What fraction of one whole does each column show?

Shade the first four columns of the other square. What is the total shaded now?
Start from the bottom and shade five small squares in the next column.
How much is shaded now? What number is now shown by the shaded parts?

How many hundredths are in one whole? How do you know?

Step Up 1. Each large square represents one whole. Write the missing numbers to describe the shaded part of each large square.

a.

___3___ tenths plus

___2___ hundredths

___32___ hundredths

b.

_____ tenths plus

_____ hundredths

_____ hundredths

c.

_____ tenths plus

_____ hundredths

_____ hundredths

d.

_____ tenths _____ hundredths

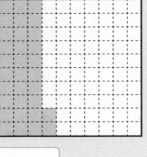

_____ hundredths

e.

_____ tenths _____ hundredths

_____ hundredths

© ORIGO Education

2. Shade each large square to match the description. Then write **how much more** needs to be shaded to make one whole.

a. 2 tenths plus
4 hundredths

_____ tenths plus

_____ hundredths

b. 4 tenths plus
9 hundredths

_____ tenths plus

_____ hundredth

c. 9 tenths plus
5 hundredths

_____ tenths plus

_____ hundredths

d. 0 tenths plus
3 hundredths

_____ tenths plus

_____ hundredths

e. 6 tenths plus
0 hundredths

_____ tenths plus

_____ hundredths

f. 4 tenths plus
15 hundredths

_____ tenths plus

_____ hundredths

Step Ahead

Draw lines to match the numbers.
Some numbers do not have a match.

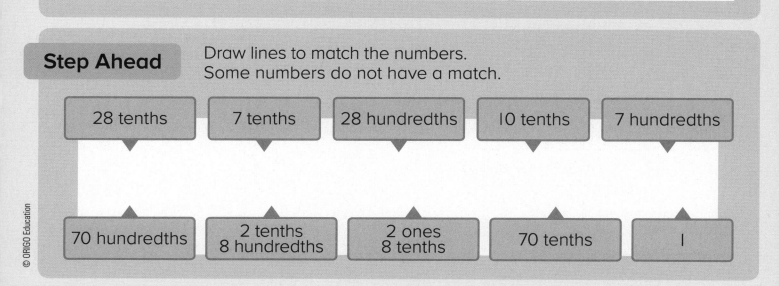

| 28 tenths | 7 tenths | 28 hundredths | 10 tenths | 7 hundredths |

| 70 hundredths | 2 tenths 8 hundredths | 2 ones 8 tenths | 70 tenths | 1 |

Step In

Each large square represents one whole.

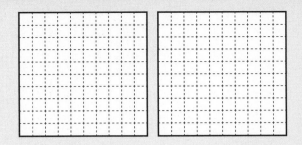

How can you color them to show **one and 76 hundredths** without counting each hundredth?

I would color all the first square to show one whole. Then I'd color 7 columns to show 7 tenths, and color 6 small squares to show 6 hundredths.

Write the number above on these two expanders.

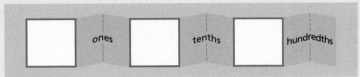 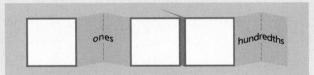

Which expander helps you to read the number? Why?

Which digit is in the tenths place? ... hundredths place?

Look at this place-value chart.

What do you notice about the places on either side of the ones place?

Write one and seventy-six hundredths on the chart.

Ten Thousands	Thousands	Hundreds	Tens	Ones	tenths	hundredths		
				•				

Step Up

1. Each large square is one whole. Color the squares to show the number. Then write the number on the expanders and as a mixed number.

two and twenty-eight hundredths

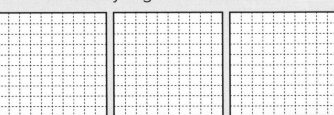 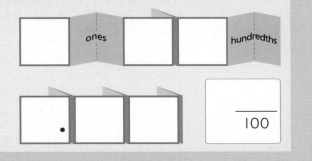

_____
100

2. Complete the missing parts. Each large square is one whole.

a.

ones [ ] . [ ] hundredths

[ ] . [ ] [ ] — / 100

b.

2 ones 9 3 hundredths

[ ] . [ ] [ ] — / 100

c.

ones [ ] . [ ] hundredths

1 . 4 7 — / 100

d.

ones [ ] . [ ] hundredths

[ ] . [ ] [ ] 1 85 / 100

Step Ahead Read the clues. Write a matching number on the expander.

a. I am greater than five and less than seven. I have more in the tenths place than in the hundredths place. I have more in the ones place than in the tenths place.

ones tenths hundredths

b. I am less than nine and greater than four. The digit in the tenths place is a multiple of 3. The digit in the hundredths place is greater than the digit in the ones place.

ones tenths hundredths

Think and Solve Write how you can use **both** of these buckets to get exactly 10 liters of water into the tub.

Buckets

 4 L

 7 L

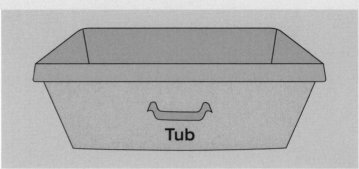
Tub

Words at Work Imagine another student was away from school when you were learning about decimal fractions. Write in words how you would explain the numbers to them.

Ongoing Practice

I. Complete each of these.

FROM 4.9.10

a.
3 lb

$\boxed{\text{is equivalent to}}$

_____ oz

b.
12 lb

$\boxed{\text{is equivalent to}}$

_____ oz

c.
$2\frac{1}{2}$ lb

$\boxed{\text{is equivalent to}}$

_____ oz

d.
$4\frac{1}{2}$ lb

$\boxed{\text{is equivalent to}}$

_____ oz

e.
20 lb

$\boxed{\text{is equivalent to}}$

_____ oz

f.
$1\frac{1}{4}$ lb

$\boxed{\text{is equivalent to}}$

_____ oz

2. Complete the missing parts. Each large square is one whole.

FROM 4.10.4

a.

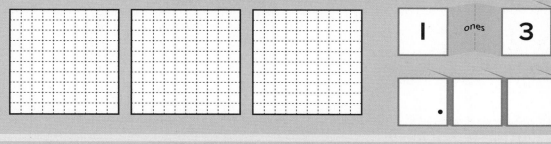

1 ones   3   9 hundredths

.

$1\frac{39}{100}$

b.

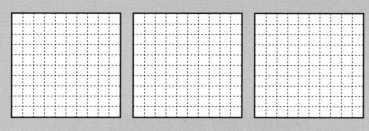

2 ones   4   6 hundredths

.

___

Preparing for Module II

Solve each problem. Show your thinking.

a. Ang bought 4 shirts for $22 each. How much did he spend?

$_____

b. Natalie bought 3 towels that cost $12 each. How much did she spend?

$_____

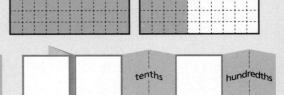

Step In   Each large square represents one whole. How much has been shaded?

Write the amount on each expander below.

How do these match the expanders above?

$$\frac{137}{100}$$ $$1 + \frac{37}{100}$$ $$\frac{13}{10} + \frac{7}{100}$$

What numbers are shaded below?

How will you write each number on the expander?

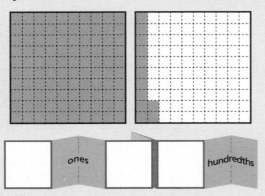   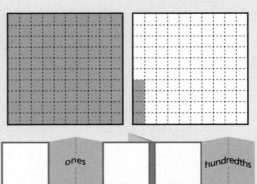

Step Up   I. Each large square represents one whole.
Complete the missing parts.

a.

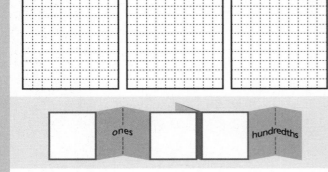

two and five hundredths

b.

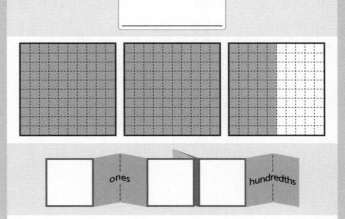

2. Read each number name. Then write the matching number on the expander.

a.

two and fourteen hundredths

b.

six and two hundredths

c.

ninety-four hundredths

d.

four and twenty hundredths

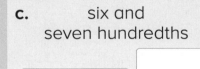

3. Write each number in words.

a. 3.19 _____

b. 9.40 _____

c. 7.06 _____

d. 12.15 _____

4. Write the matching decimal fraction and mixed number.

a. six and seventeen hundredths	**b.** six and seventy hundredths	**c.** six and seven hundredths

Step Ahead Circle the numbers that are the same as 705 hundredths.

0.705 $7\frac{5}{10}$ 7.05 $7\frac{5}{100}$ 0.75

Decimal fractions: Writing in expanded form

Step In   Read the number on the expander.

What is the value of each 4 on the expander?

What is the value of the 6?

> Just like whole numbers, decimal fractions can be recorded in expanded form.

Write the missing numbers.

(⬚ × 1) + (⬚ × 0.1) + (⬚ × 0.01)

Dwane wrote a different decimal fraction in expanded form.

(1 × 0.1) + (7 × 1) + (9 × 0.01)

What do you notice?

What decimal fraction did he expand?

Write the decimal fraction on the expander.

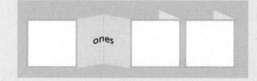

Step Up   I.   Write the missing numbers to match the expander.

a.
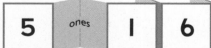

(⬚ × 1) + (⬚ × 0.1) + (⬚ × 0.01)

b.

5 ones 1 6

(⬚ × 1) + (⬚ × 0.1) + (⬚ × 0.01)

c.

7 ones 0 5

(⬚ × 1) + (⬚ × 0.1) + (⬚ × 0.01)

2. Write each decimal fraction in expanded form.

a. 6.85 _____

b. 8.18 _____

c. 6.03 _____

d. 1.80 _____

e. 0.75 _____

3. Write the decimal fraction that has been expanded.

a. (2 × 1) + (5 × 0.1) + (2 × 0.01)

b. (8 × 1) + (4 × 0.1) + (1 × 0.01)

c. (5 × 1) + (6 × 0.1) + (7 × 0.01)

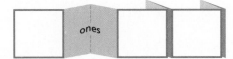

d. (6 × 0.1) + (7 × 0.01)

Step Ahead

Look carefully at the decimal fraction that has been expanded. Then write the decimal fraction on the expander.

a. (9 × 0.01) + (4 × 1) + (7 × 0.1)

b. (6 × 0.1) + (1 × 0.01) + (5 × 1)

c. (4 × 0.1) + (7 × 1) + (2 × 0.01)

d. (9 × 0.01) + (2 × 1)

Computation Practice   Which animal can last longer without water than a camel?

★ Complete the equations. Find each quotient in the grid below and cross out the letter above. Then write the remaining letters at the bottom of the page.

132 ÷ 3 = ___	316 ÷ 4 = ___	485 ÷ 5 = ___
365 ÷ 5 = ___	522 ÷ 3 = ___	252 ÷ 4 = ___
224 ÷ 4 = ___	185 ÷ 5 = ___	411 ÷ 3 = ___
429 ÷ 3 = ___	544 ÷ 4 = ___	375 ÷ 5 = ___
225 ÷ 5 = ___	501 ÷ 3 = ___	328 ÷ 4 = ___
584 ÷ 4 = ___	312 ÷ 3 = ___	256 ÷ 4 = ___
213 ÷ 3 = ___	336 ÷ 4 = ___	

B	A	T	H	O	R	S	E
56	39	44	143	79	65	37	45
E	C	H	I	D	N	A	S
75	63	146	64	97	71	144	136
E	L	E	P	H	A	N	T
73	82	84	104	174	137	167	83

Write the letters in order from the ✳ to the bottom-right corner.

 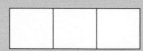

Ongoing Practice

1. Use the standard subtraction algorithm to calculate the exact difference.

a.

Th	H	T	O
4	6	3	7
− 1	4	8	5

b.

TTh	Th	H	T	O
1	2	5	7	3
−	6	1	4	8

c.

TTh	Th	H	T	O
3	4	5	1	6
− 1	1	8	9	3

2. Write the decimal fractions that have been expanded.

a. $(3 \times 1) + (4 \times 0.1) + (7 \times 0.01)$

b. $(9 \times 1) + (6 \times 0.01)$

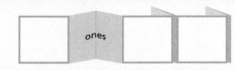

c. $(2 \times 1) + (1 \times 0.1) + (1 \times 0.01)$

d. $(5 \times 1) + (8 \times 0.1) + (0 \times 0.01)$

Preparing for Module 11

Double one number and halve the other. Then write the products.

a. $15 \times 6 = \boxed{}$

is the same value as

___ × ___ = ___

b. $35 \times 6 = \boxed{}$

is the same value as

___ × ___ = ___

c. $3 \times 22 = \boxed{}$

is the same value as

___ × ___ = ___

d. $32 \times 5 = \boxed{}$

is the same value as

___ × ___ = ___

e. $18 \times 5 = \boxed{}$

is the same value as

___ × ___ = ___

f. $8 \times 45 = \boxed{}$

is the same value as

___ × ___ = ___

Decimal fractions: Locating tenths and hundredths on a number line

The distance between each whole number on these number lines is one whole.

What number is the arrow pointing to? What helped you figure it out?

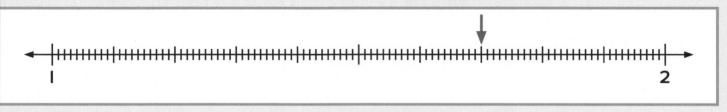

What other decimal fraction describes that position? How do you know?

Look where the top arrow is pointing. Which two decimal fractions describe that position?

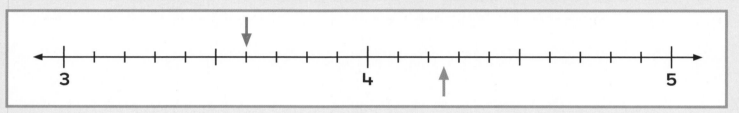

What number do you think the bottom arrow is pointing to? How could you figure it out?

Step Up

1. The distance between each whole number is one whole. Write the decimal fraction shown by each arrow. Think carefully before you write.

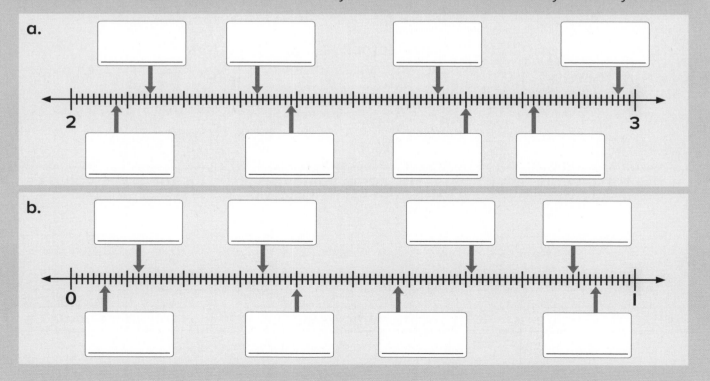

© ORIGO Education

2. The distance between each whole number is one whole. Draw a line to join each number to its approximate position on the number line. Be as accurate as possible.

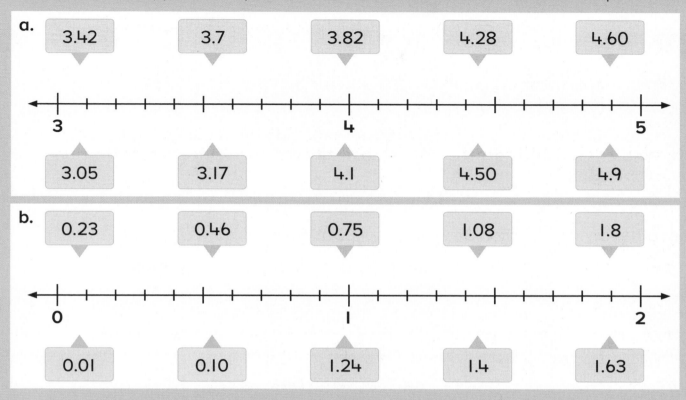

a.

| 3.42 | 3.7 | 3.82 | 4.28 | 4.60 |

3   4   5

| 3.05 | 3.17 | 4.1 | 4.50 | 4.9 |

b.

| 0.23 | 0.46 | 0.75 | 1.08 | 1.8 |

0   1   2

| 0.01 | 0.10 | 1.24 | 1.4 | 1.63 |

Step Ahead

Race times can be recorded in whole seconds, tenths, and hundredths of a second. Draw arrows and write **initials** to show the approximate position of each athlete's time. Write above or below the number line. The first one has been done for you.

2016 Olympic Games Men's 200 Meters

Athlete	Time (s)	Athlete	Time (s)
Usain Bolt	19.78	Churandy Martina	20.13
Andre De Grasse	20.02	LaShawn Merritt	20.19
Christophe Lemaitre	20.12	Alfonso Edward	20.23
Adam Gemili	20.12	Ramil Guliyev	20.43

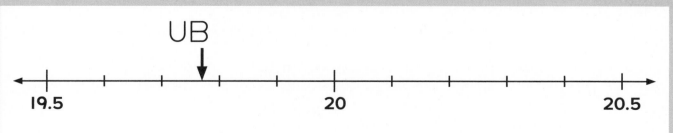

UB

19.5   20   20.5

Step In   Look at these six decimal fractions.

	A	B	C	D	E	F
	3.41	3.38	2.6	3.8	3.04	2.43

Which number is greater, C or F?
How could you figure it out?

Gloria thought it would be easier to compare the numbers if they had the same denominator. How should she change the numbers? Do you need to change only one number, or both numbers?

> I would think about where the numbers would be on a number line.

Between which two whole numbers are the numbers C and F?
Write the whole numbers and the numbers C and F on this number line.

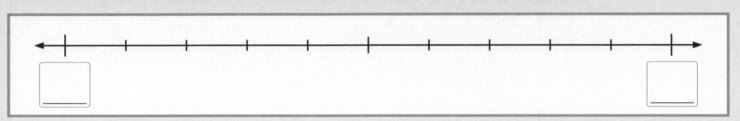

> I would think about the place value of each number.

H	T	O	t	h

Write each number in these place-value charts.
How do the charts help you figure out the greater number?

H	T	O	t	h

Step Up   1. Write < or > to make each statement true. Use what you know about equivalence to help you.

a. 0.5 ◯ 0.08   b. 0.7 ◯ 0.07   c. 1.25 ◯ 1.4   d. 2.75 ◯ 27.5

e. 1.75 ◯ 2.7   f. 4.1 ◯ 4.01   g. 2.3 ◯ 2.03   h. 2.01 ◯ 5.9

© ORIGO Education

These eight decimal fractions are between 1 and 4. Use the data in the table to answer Questions 2 and 3. Use the number line and what you know about equivalence to help you.

P	Q	R	S	T	U	V	W
1.96	2.91	3.4	3.12	2.19	2.03	3.2	2.3

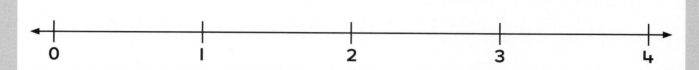

2. Write the number from the table. Then write **<** or **>** to complete each statement.

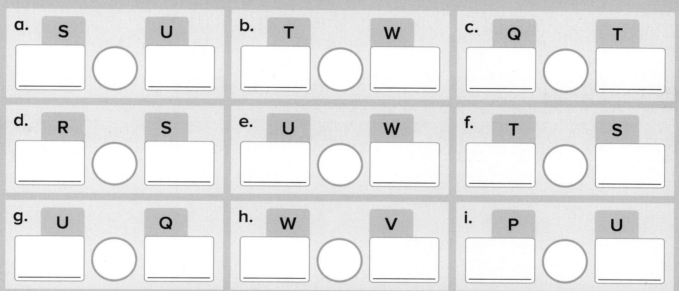

a. S ◯ U

b. T ◯ W

c. Q ◯ T

d. R ◯ S

e. U ◯ W

f. T ◯ S

g. U ◯ Q

h. W ◯ V

i. P ◯ U

3. Write the decimal fractions in order from **least** to **greatest**.

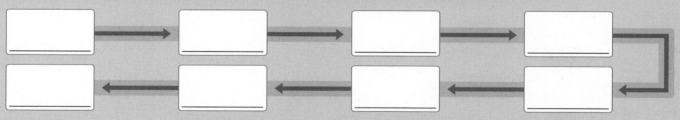

Step Ahead   Write these numbers in order from **greatest** to **least**.

0.2	0.58	0.6	1.4	1.07	2.00	0.09

greatest ___ ___ ___ ___ ___ ___ least

Think and Solve

a. Lisa's secret number is _____ .

b. Liam's secret number is _____ .

c. Terri's secret number is _____ .

d. Reece's secret number is _____ .

Clues

Lisa's secret number is 5 more than Liam's number.

Liam's secret number is twice Terri's number.

Terri's secret number is 6 less than Reece's number.

Reece's secret number is a multiple of 2, 3, 4, 6, 8, and 12. It has 4 ones.

Words at Work

Write the answer for each clue in the grid. Use words from the list. Some words are not used.

Clues Across

2. The decimal ___ shows the ones place.

3. The hundredths place is ___ places to the right of the ones place.

5. A decimal fraction is a ___ that is written with no visible denominator.

6. Five tenths ___ six hundredths can be written as fifty-six hundredths.

Clues Down

1. Sixty-___ tenths has the same value as 6.4.

2. The ones ___ is just left of the tenths place.

4. A zero is used in the ___ place when the amount is less than 1.

| right |
| four |
| fraction |
| and |
| point |
| two |
| left |
| ones |
| plus |
| decimal |
| three |
| place |

© ORIGO Education

Ongoing Practice

I. Use the standard subtraction algorithm to calculate these.

a.

TTh	Th	H	T	O
3	1	4	6	2
− 1	5	1	7	5

b.

TTh	Th	H	T	O
4	0	7	5	9
− 2	3	0	6	4

c.

TTh	Th	H	T	O
2	7	4	8	2
− 1	3	6	4	5

d.

3	5	7	2	9
−	8	3	7	5

e.

3	9	6	4	5
− 1	6	3	8	7

f.

7	5	2	8	1
− 2	7	1	5	9

2. The distance between each whole number is one whole. Draw a line to join each number to its position on the number line. Be as accurate as possible.

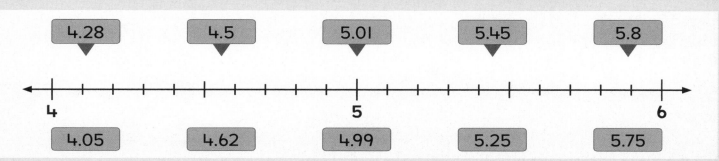

Preparing for Module II

Complete these to show pairs of possible factors.

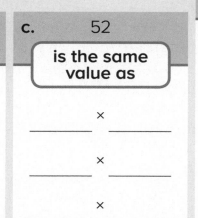

a.   32
is the same value as

_____ × _____

_____ × _____

_____ × _____

b.   44
is the same value as

_____ × _____

_____ × _____

_____ × _____

c.   52
is the same value as

_____ × _____

_____ × _____

_____ × _____

d.   64
is the same value as

_____ × _____

_____ × _____

_____ × _____

Step In

Ruben and Karen are going on a 5-km fun run.

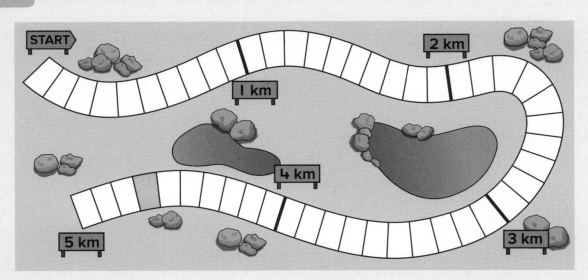

How has each kilometer been divided?
What fraction of one kilometer does the orange part show?

Shade 1.3 km of the track from the start.
What is two-tenths of a kilometer more? How can you figure it out?

Use decimal fractions to write an equation that shows the total.

☐ + ☐ = ☐

Use mixed numbers and common fractions to write a different equation that shows the total.

☐ + ☐ = ☐

On another fun run, the total distance is 10 km.

If you were at the mark for 5.3 km, where will you be after you run 2.4 km farther along the track? How can you figure it out?

I would add the ones together, then add the tenths together, then add the totals. I use the same strategy for adding two-digit whole numbers.

It's like adding mixed numbers. I would add the whole numbers and fractions separately, then add the totals together.

I could start with 5.3, then add 2, and add 0.4.

Step Up

1. Calculate the total distance for each of these.

a.
3.4 km + 2.3 km = [____] km

b.
2.1 km + 3.5 km = [____] km

c.
2.7 km + 4.2 km = [____] km

d.
6.3 km + 1.4 km = [____] km

e.
6.1 km + 2.3 km = [____] km

f.
3.2 km + 3.5 km = [____] km

g.
1.6 km + 4.2 km = [____] km

h.
4.5 km + 1.4 km = [____] km

i.
5.3 km + 2.3 km = [____] km

j.
5.4 km + 3.5 km = [____] km

2. There are checkpoints located every 3.1 km along a fun run.

   a. Write how far each checkpoint is from the start.

	Checkpoint 1	Checkpoint 2	Checkpoint 3	Checkpoint 4	Checkpoint 5	
START	[____]	[____]	[____]	[____]	[____]	FINISH

   b. The finish is located 1.5 km after the last checkpoint.

   How long is the fun run? [____] km

Step Ahead

Maka and Lillian ran a relay. Maka ran the first 3.1 kilometers, then Lillian ran the last 3.3 kilometers.

a. Did they run greater than or less than 6.05 kilometers in total? [____]

b. Write how you know. [____]

[____]

Decimal fractions: Adding hundredths

Step In

A new downspout is being made to attach to the side of a building. This sketch shows the pipes that are needed.

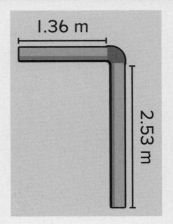

1.36 m

2.53 m

How could you calculate the total length of straight pipe?

I would add the ones together, then the tenths, then the hundredths.

These two items are needed for the downspout.
What is their total cost? How could you figure it out?

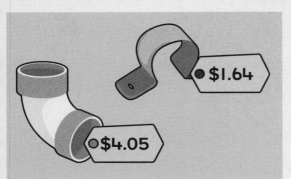

$1.64

$4.05

It's easy to think about this. The whole numbers are dollars and the fractions are cents.

Step Up

1. Add the lengths and write the total. Show your thinking.

a.
4.32 m + 3.65 m = _____ m

b.
3.72 m + 3.15 m = _____ m

c.
1.65 m + 0.23 m = _____ m

d.
2.84 m + 5.03 m = _____ m

2. Write the total cost. Show your thinking.

a.

$3.56 $1.42

$_____

b.
$5.24 $3.45

$_____

c.
$2.06 $2.31

$_____

d.

$4.20 $1.50

$_____

e.
$3.71 $5.00

$_____

f.
$0.65 $1.24

$_____

Step Ahead   Write each decimal fraction as a mixed number or common fraction then write the total. The first numbers have been done for you.

a. 4.35 + 1.62	**b.** 2.17 + 3.41	**c.** 1.62 + 1.05
$4\frac{35}{100} + 1\frac{62}{100} = \boxed{}$		

d. 0.02 + 0.07	**e.** 1.40 + 0.08	**f.** 0.04 + 0.60

Computation Practice   What sort of ring is always square?

★ Use a ruler to draw a straight line to the correct total. The line will pass through a letter. Write each letter below its matching total in the grid.

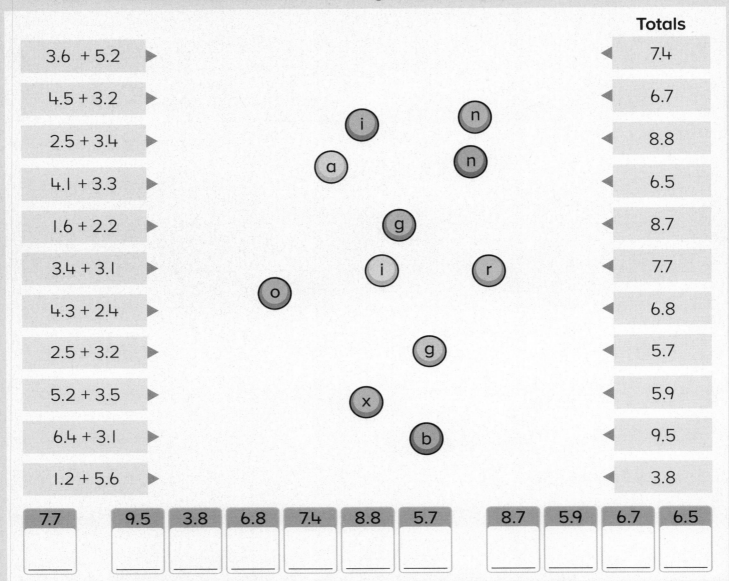

Totals

3.6 + 5.2 ▶	◀ 7.4
4.5 + 3.2 ▶	◀ 6.7
2.5 + 3.4 ▶	◀ 8.8
4.1 + 3.3 ▶	◀ 6.5
1.6 + 2.2 ▶	◀ 8.7
3.4 + 3.1 ▶	◀ 7.7
4.3 + 2.4 ▶	◀ 6.8
2.5 + 3.2 ▶	◀ 5.7
5.2 + 3.5 ▶	◀ 5.9
6.4 + 3.1 ▶	◀ 9.5
1.2 + 5.6 ▶	◀ 3.8

7.7	9.5	3.8	6.8	7.4	8.8	5.7	8.7	5.9	6.7	6.5

Write the totals for these.

14.6 + 4.2 = _____   11.7 + 6.1 = _____   3.2 + 31.6 = _____

4.8 + 23.1 = _____   2.4 + 25.5 = _____   1.4 + 24.3 = _____

3.2 + 15.3 = _____   32.6 + 2.2 = _____   31.4 + 3.5 = _____

© ORIGO Education

Ongoing Practice

I. Use the standard addition algorithm to calculate these.

a.
```
   3  6  1  5
   4  0  7  2
+  1  4  3  1
_____
```

b.
```
   2  8  0  0
   6  1  7  5
+  3  4  2  9
_____
```

c.
```
   2  6  3  4  7
+  1  3  5  9  5
_____
```

d.
```
   3  5  0  6
   7  2  8  1
+  1  4  3  0
_____
```

2. Calculate the total distance for each of these.

a.
3.2 km + 4.5 km = [   ] km

b.
5.1 km + 2.7 km = [   ] km

c.
2.6 km + 1.3 km = [   ] km

d.
2.3 km + 6.4 km = [   ] km

e.
4.5 km + 2.4 km = [   ] km

f.
4.2 km + 2.6 km = [   ] km

g.
6.3 km + 3.5 km = [   ] km

h.
1.6 km + 4.2 km = [   ] km

Preparing for Module II

Look at the diagram. Use the clues to calculate the size of each angle. Do not use a protractor. Show your thinking.

Clues

- Angle **AOC** is 90°.
- Angle **AOD** is 120°.
- Angle **AOB** is 30°.
- Angle **AOE** is 180°.

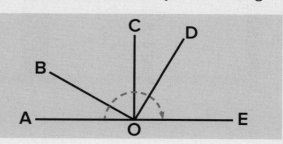

Angle **DOE** is [   ]°

Angle **COE** is [   ]°

Angle **BOD** is [   ]°

Step In

Ruth drew these large squares to help calculate the total of 0.4 and 0.23.

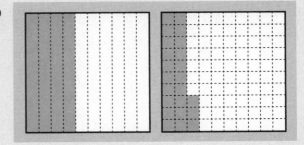

How could you use the squares to help you?

Jamar wrote the numbers as common fractions to help him think about the problem.

He realized the denominators were different, and knew that adding fractions was easier when they had the same denominator.

$\frac{4}{10}$ $\frac{23}{100}$

How could he change the fractions?

Selena thought about the value of each place and knew if she added like places she would find the total.

The decimal point tells me where the ones place is. Then it's easy.

What helps her identify the places correctly?

How would you use each of these methods to calculate the total of 2.05 and 0.8?

Step Up

1. Complete each equation. You can use the large squares to help you. Each large square is one whole.

a. 0.5 + 0.34 = _____

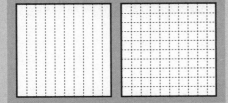

b. 0.3 + 0.25 = _____

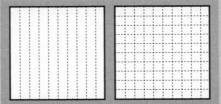

c. 1.0 + 0.43 = _____

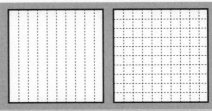

d. 0.1 + 0.11 = _____

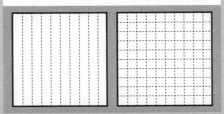

e. 0.6 + 0.20 = _____

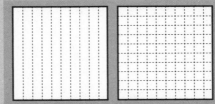

f. 0.4 + 0.03 = _____

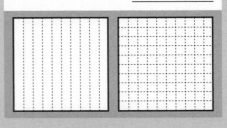

2. Use what you know about equivalence to calculate each total. Show your thinking on page 394.

a. $\frac{6}{10} + \frac{15}{100} = $ ☐

b. $\frac{5}{10} + \frac{5}{100} = $ ☐

c. $\frac{2}{10} + \frac{45}{100} = $ ☐

d. $\frac{8}{10} + \frac{12}{100} = $ ☐

e. $2\frac{1}{10} + \frac{30}{100} = $ ☐

f. $\frac{1}{10} + 2\frac{7}{100} = $ ☐

g. $1\frac{14}{100} + \frac{6}{10} = $ ☐

h. $\frac{2}{100} + \frac{9}{10} = $ ☐

i. $3\frac{33}{100} + \frac{4}{10} = $ ☐

3. Choose six totals from Question 2. Write each as a decimal fraction.

a. _____ b. _____ c. _____ d. _____ e. _____ f. _____

4. Show each decimal fraction as the sum of three numbers.

a. $1.34 = $ 1 $+$ 0.3 $+$ 0.04

b. $2.47 = $ ☐ $+$ ☐ $+$ ☐

c. $1.45 = $ ☐ $+$ ☐ $+$ ☐

d. $2.96 = $ ☐ $+$ ☐ $+$ ☐

e. $0.67 = $ ☐ $+$ ☐ $+$ ☐

f. $1.50 = $ ☐ $+$ ☐ $+$ ☐

Step Ahead

Figure out which pairs of numbers add to a total that is a whole number. Use the same color to show matching pairs. Some numbers have no match.

| 0.95 | 0.6 | 0.90 | 2.0 |

| 0.1 | 0.09 | 1.2 | 0.50 | 2.40 |

| 0.8 | 3.5 | 1.05 | 0.01 |

ORIGO Stepping Stones · Grade 4 · 10.11

© ORIGO Education

Step In

Connor is wrapping two packages to send. He knows the post office closes in half an hour. One package weighs 5.2 lb and the other weighs a quarter of a pound.

What is the total mass of the packages? _____ lb

What information in the story is necessary to help you answer the question?

What steps will you follow to calculate the answer?

I need to write $\frac{1}{4}$ of a pound as a decimal fraction.

Step Up

1. Figure out the answer to each problem. Show your thinking.

a. A tub of rice weighs 1.75 kg. More rice is added to make 2.05 kg. How much extra rice was put in the tub?

_____ kg

b. Vishaya rides 4.6 miles. Jacob rides 8.3 miles more than Vishaya. How far does Jacob ride?

_____ mi

c. Kettle A holds 1.7 liters. Kettle B holds 2.25 liters. How much more water does Kettle B hold?

_____ L

d. There is $2.48 in a piggy bank. If you put in three more dimes, how much money will there be inside?

$_____

2. Solve each problem. Show your thinking.

a. On Monday, Morgan runs $3\frac{1}{4}$ km.
On Tuesday, she runs 2.3 km.
On Wednesday, she runs 4.1 km.
How far does she run in total
on Monday and Wednesday?

_____ km

b. Antonio pours $\frac{3}{4}$ of a liter of juice
into a pitcher. There is now 0.9 liters
of juice in the pitcher. How much
juice was in the pitcher before?

_____ L

c. Dorothy weighs 4.2 kg less
than her brother. She weighs
25.7 kg. How much does her
brother weigh?

_____ kg

d. Kasem has $2 to buy some nuts.
The red bag costs $0.57, the blue bag
costs $1.62, and the brown bag costs
$1.20. Which two bags can he buy?

_____

What is the total cost? $ _____

Step Ahead

a. Which frozen yogurt is the better buy?

_____

b. Write how you know.

_____

_____

_____

FROZEN YOGURT 1.75 qt   FROZEN YOGURT 1.5 qt

$4.99 $4.99

Think and Solve

Imagine you tossed a coin onto each target and multiplied the two numbers.

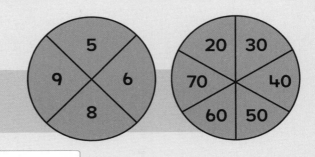

a. What is the greatest product you can get? ☐

b. What is the least product you can get? ☐

c. Write an equation to show how you can get 180?

☐ × ☐ = **180**

d. Write an equation to show how you can get 300.

☐ × ☐ = **300**

e. Write equations to show two ways you can get 240.

☐ × ☐ = **240**   ☐ × ☐ = **240**

Words at Work

Write a word problem that involves adding two decimal fractions. Then write how you would solve the problem.

_____

_____

_____

_____

_____

_____

_____

_____

Ongoing Practice

I. Complete these.

a.

```
    3   4   6   1   8
+   1   6   7   4   3
_____
```

b.

```
    4   7   6   0
    3   1   0   8
+   2   2   9   5
_____
```

c.

```
    2   7   3   0   6
+   1   5   2   9   8
_____
```

2. Write the total cost. Show your thinking.

a.   ○$2.55   ○$3.20

$_____

b.   ○$1.42   ○$5.35

$_____

c.   ○$3.15   ○$2.70

$_____

d.   ○$4.25   ○$2.44

$_____

Preparing for Module 11

Draw a line to split each shape into halves.

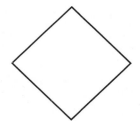 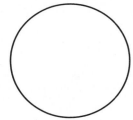 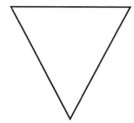 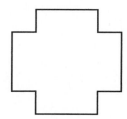

Multiplication: Introducing the standard algorithm with two-digit numbers (regrouping tens)

Step In The dimensions for a courtyard are 32 ft × 3 ft.

How could you calculate the area?

Rita drew a rectangle to represent the courtyard. She then split the rectangle into parts that are easier to multiply.

Write the area of each part.

3

30   2

Jerome used the standard multiplication algorithm to calculate the area. He followed these steps.

Think about the numbers that are multiplied in each step. How do they match each of the partial products in Rita's diagram?

Step 1		Step 2	
T	O	T	O
3	2	3	2
×	3	×	3
	6	9	6

Another courtyard measures 7 ft × 21 ft.

Write the partial products in the diagram to help calculate the area.

Look at the steps for the standard multiplication algorithm.

7

20   1

What numbers are multiplied in each step?

How do the numbers in each step, match each partial product?

What number does the 14 actually represent?

Step 1			Step 2		
H	T	O	H	T	O
	2	1		2	1
×		7	×		7
		7	1	4	7

l. Estimate each product. Then use the standard multiplication algorithm to calculate the exact answer.

a. Estimate

```
    T   O
    2 | 3
×   ──┼──
      | 3
    ──┼──
      |
```

b. Estimate

```
    T   O
    2 | 1
×   ──┼──
      | 4
    ──┼──
      |
```

c. Estimate

```
    T   O
    3 | 3
×   ──┼──
      | 3
    ──┼──
      |
```

d. Estimate

```
    T   O
    2 | 2
×   ──┼──
      | 3
    ──┼──
      |
```

2. Complete each of these.

a. Estimate

```
  H   T   O
      3 | 2
×   ──┼───┼──
        | 4
    ──┼───┼──
      |   |
```

b. Estimate

```
  H   T   O
      5 | 3
×   ──┼───┼──
        | 3
    ──┼───┼──
      |   |
```

c. Estimate

```
  H   T   O
      2 | 1
×   ──┼───┼──
        | 6
    ──┼───┼──
      |   |
```

d. Estimate

```
  H   T   O
      4 | 2
×   ──┼───┼──
        | 3
    ──┼───┼──
      |   |
```

e. Estimate

```
  H   T   O
      3 | 1
×   ──┼───┼──
        | 5
    ──┼───┼──
      |   |
```

f. Estimate

```
  H   T   O
      4 | 1
×   ──┼───┼──
        | 3
    ──┼───┼──
      |   |
```

g. Estimate

```
  H   T   O
      6 | 2
×   ──┼───┼──
        | 4
    ──┼───┼──
      |   |
```

h. Estimate

```
  H   T   O
      5 | 1
×   ──┼───┼──
        | 9
    ──┼───┼──
      |   |
```

Choose one of the problems above that you could solve using a different strategy. Explain how you would calculate the answer.

Step In

Robert visits the penguin enclosure at the zoo.
The enclosure is rectangular in shape.
The short side is 4 yards long. The long side is 23 yards.

What is the area of the penguin enclosure?

Robert draws this picture.

Write the partial products in the diagram to help calculate the area.

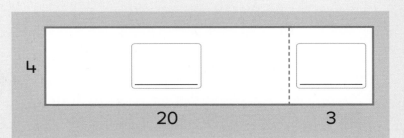

The standard multiplication algorithm could also be used to calculate the answer.

What numbers are multiplied in each step?

How do the numbers in each step match each of the partial products above?

In Step 1, what does the number 1 in the tens column mean? How is it used in Step 2?

Step 1

```
    T   O
    |
    2   3
×       4
─────────
        2
```

Step 2

```
    T   O
    |
    2   3
×       4
─────────
    9   2
```

Step Up

1. Write the partial products in the diagram. Then complete the standard multiplication algorithm to match.

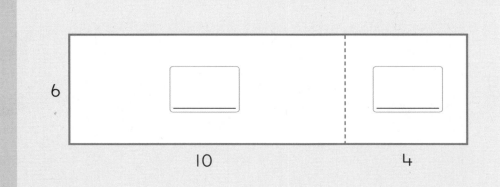

```
    T   O
    |   4
×       6
─────────
```

2. Estimate each product. Then use the standard multiplication algorithm to calculate the exact answer.

a. Estimate

T	O
3	2
×	3

b. Estimate

T	O
2	2
×	4

c. Estimate

T	O
4	3
×	2

d. Estimate

T	O
2	1
×	3

e. Estimate

2	7
×	3

f. Estimate

1	9
×	4

g. Estimate

1	7
×	5

h. Estimate

1	3
×	7

i. Estimate

1	6
×	6

j. Estimate

2	9
×	3

k. Estimate

1	9
×	5

l. Estimate

1	8
×	4

Step Ahead

Look at each card below. Write **M** on the card that matches the thinking used in this standard multiplication algorithm.

$6 \times 2 = 12$
$6 \times 3 = 18$

$6 \times 2 = 12$
$6 \times 30 = 180$

$6 \times 20 = 120$
$6 \times 3 = 18$

	3	2
×		6
1	9	2

Maintaining concepts and skills

Computation Practice

★ Complete these facts as fast as you can. Use the classroom clock to time yourself.

Time Taken: ______

start

40 ÷ 5 = ___	32 ÷ 8 = ___	12 ÷ 6 = ___
56 ÷ 7 = ___	63 ÷ 9 = ___	35 ÷ 7 = ___
45 ÷ 9 = ___	64 ÷ 8 = ___	27 ÷ 3 = ___
10 ÷ 5 = ___	81 ÷ 9 = ___	42 ÷ 6 = ___
9 ÷ 1 = ___	20 ÷ 5 = ___	36 ÷ 4 = ___
6 ÷ 1 = ___	54 ÷ 6 = ___	48 ÷ 8 = ___
18 ÷ 2 = ___	24 ÷ 4 = ___	72 ÷ 8 = ___

finish

Ongoing Practice

1. On these number lines, the distance between each whole number is one whole. Write the decimal fraction that is shown by each arrow.

a.

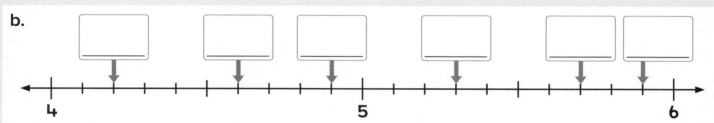

b.

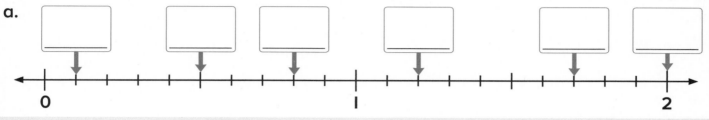

FROM 4.10.2

2. Estimate each product. Then use the standard multiplication algorithm to calculate the exact answer.

FROM 4.11.2

a. Estimate	b. Estimate	c. Estimate	d. Estimate

T	O
2	1
×	3

T	O
1	4
×	4

T	O
1	8
×	5

T	O
1	5
×	4

Preparing for Module 12

Draw the next picture in this pattern.

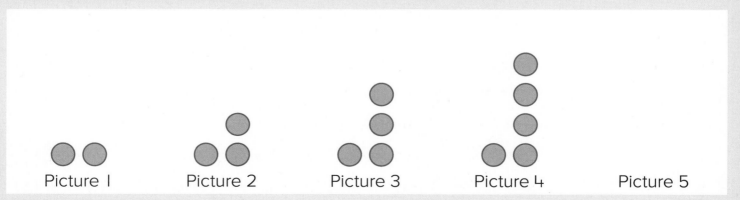

Picture 1   Picture 2   Picture 3   Picture 4   Picture 5

Step In

How would you calculate the total cost of buying eight tickets?

Do you think the total cost will be more or less than $200?

$32
= ADMIT ONE =

Complete the diagram to show one way to calculate the total cost.

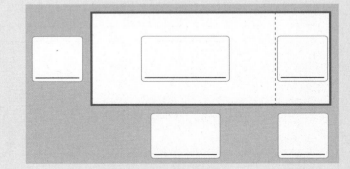

You could also use the standard multiplication algorithm.

What numbers are multiplied in each step?

How do the steps match each of the partial products?

In Step 1, what does the numeral 1 in the tens column mean?
How is it used in Step 2?

Step 1

H	T	O
	1	
	3	2
×		8
		6

Step 2

H	T	O
	1	
	3	2
×		8
2	5	6

Step Up

1. Write the partial products in the diagram. Then complete the standard multiplication algorithm to match.

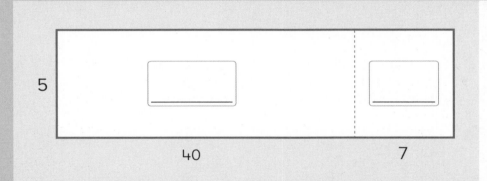

5

40   7

H	T	O
	4	7
×		5

2. Estimate each product. Then use the standard multiplication algorithm to calculate the exact answer.

a. Estimate

H	T	O
	3	1
×		3

b. Estimate

H	T	O
	2	4
×		3

c. Estimate

H	T	O
	1	7
×		5

d. Estimate

H	T	O
	3	4
×		4

e. Estimate

	2	6
×		3

f. Estimate

	2	9
×		4

g. Estimate

	3	7
×		5

h. Estimate

	5	3
×		8

i. Estimate

	3	6
×		7

j. Estimate

	4	9
×		8

k. Estimate

	3	8
×		9

l. Estimate

	5	7
×		6

Step Ahead   Choose one of the problems above that you could use a doubling strategy to calculate the product. Show your thinking.

Multiplication: Solving word problems involving two-digit numbers

Step In

The local sports team needs to buy eight team shirts.

How could you calculate the total cost?

> I could use the partial-products strategy, the double-and-halve strategy, or I could double double, double 45.

Amber used the standard multiplication algorithm to calculate the total cost.

Which method do you think is the easiest to use with these numbers? Why?

The team also needs to buy nine shorts.

Which method would you use to calculate the total cost? Why?

	H	T	O
		4	
		4	5
×			8
	3	6	0

Step Up

I. Solve each problem. Show your thinking.

a. Trophies cost $18 each. How much will 9 trophies cost?

$_____

b. Caps are $23 each and socks are $9 a pair. How much will 7 caps cost?

$_____

2. Solve each problem. Show your thinking.

a. Shirts are $39 each which is $15 less than the price of a bat. What is the total cost of 8 bats?

$_____

b. Sports bags are $28 each and balls are $13 each. What is the total cost of 9 bags and 6 balls?

$_____

c. The coach buys boots for $36 and socks for $9 for each player on the team. There are 9 players. What is the total cost?

$_____

d. There are 14 girls teams and 12 boys teams in a league. Each team has one manager and 8 players. How many players are in the league?

_____ players

Step Ahead

Look at Question 2d. Think about a different way to find the answer. Show your thinking.

_____ players

Think and Solve Look at this number. Complete the equations.

105

a. ⬜ + ⬜ = 105

b. ⬜ + ⬜ + ⬜ = 105

c. ⬜ × ⬜ = 105

d. ⬜ − ⬜ = 105

e. ⬜ ÷ ⬜ = 105

f. ⬜ × ⬜ × ⬜ = 105

Words at Work You could use the standard multiplication algorithm to calculate the product of 57 × 5. Write about **two** other ways you could calculate the product.

Ongoing Practice

1. Shade each large square to match the description. Then write how much more needs to be shaded to make one whole.

a. **6** tenths plus
   5 hundredths

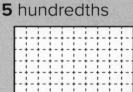

_____ tenths plus

_____ hundredths

b. **5** tenths plus
   7 hundredths

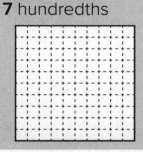

_____ tenths plus

_____ hundredths

c. **3** tenths plus
   6 hundredths

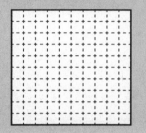

_____ tenths plus

_____ hundredths

2. Estimate each product. Then use the standard multiplication algorithm to calculate the exact answer.

a. Estimate

H	T	O
	2	9
×		3

b. Estimate

H	T	O
	2	7
×		4

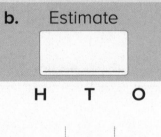

c. Estimate

H	T	O
	3	5
×		3

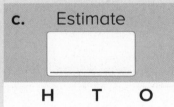

d. Estimate

H	T	O
	5	2
×		9

Preparing for Module 12   Complete these.

a.

6:58

_____ minutes to _____

b.

10:36

_____ minutes to _____

Step In

I want to lay turf in an area that measures 12 yd by 15 yd. How many square yards of turf will I need?

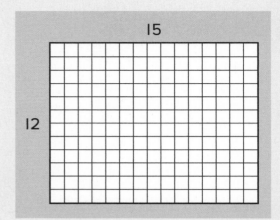

Look at this array. How could you calculate the number of square yards without counting all the squares?

There are 30 squares in two rows. 30 + 30 + 30 + 30 + 30 + 30 = 180.

You could also double and halve.
Imagine the array above is cut in half and rearranged like this.

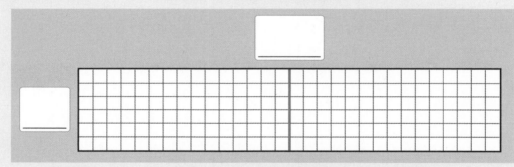

Has the total number of squares changed? Label the new dimensions.

Are these numbers easier to multiply in your head?

How could you use the double-and-halve strategy to calculate 45 × 18?

How did you decide which factor to double and which factor to halve?

Step Up

1. Double one number and halve the other to make a problem that is easier to solve. Then write the product.

a.   15 × 14

_____ × _____

15 × 14 = _____

b.   16 × 15

_____ × _____

16 × 15 = _____

c.   35 × 8

_____ × _____

35 × 8 = _____

© ORIGO Education

2. Double and halve twice to solve each of these.

a. $\quad15 \times 28$

$$\underline{\hspace{1.5cm}} \times \underline{\hspace{1.5cm}}$$

$$\underline{\hspace{1.5cm}} \times \underline{\hspace{1.5cm}}$$

$15 \times 28 = \boxed{\underline{\hspace{1.5cm}}}$

b. $\quad13 \times 16$

$$\underline{\hspace{1.5cm}} \times \underline{\hspace{1.5cm}}$$

$$\underline{\hspace{1.5cm}} \times \underline{\hspace{1.5cm}}$$

$13 \times 16 = \boxed{\underline{\hspace{1.5cm}}}$

c. $\quad28 \times 25$

$$\underline{\hspace{1.5cm}} \times \underline{\hspace{1.5cm}}$$

$$\underline{\hspace{1.5cm}} \times \underline{\hspace{1.5cm}}$$

$28 \times 25 = \boxed{\underline{\hspace{1.5cm}}}$

3. Calculate the products. Show the steps you use.

a. $\quad 25 \times 24 = \boxed{\underline{\hspace{1cm}}}$

b. $\quad 45 \times 16 = \boxed{\underline{\hspace{1cm}}}$

c. $\quad 18 \times 4 = \boxed{\underline{\hspace{1cm}}}$

d. $\quad 35 \times 16 = \boxed{\underline{\hspace{1cm}}}$

e. $\quad 12 \times 75 = \boxed{\underline{\hspace{1cm}}}$

f. $\quad 12 \times 55 = \boxed{\underline{\hspace{1cm}}}$

Step Ahead

Circle the card that you **would not** use the double-and-halve strategy to solve. Then explain your reasoning.

| 45×12 | 35×15 | 16×25 | 18×5 |

$$\underline{\hspace{15cm}}$$

$$\underline{\hspace{15cm}}$$

$$\underline{\hspace{15cm}}$$

Step In	What are the dimensions of this prism?

How could you calculate the total number of cubes?

Write an equation to show the order that you would use to multiply the dimensions.

☐ × ☐ × ☐ = ☐

What makes your equation easier to figure out?

Imagine a prism has 72 cubes on the base and is five layers high.
How would you calculate the total number of cubes?

That is 5 × 72. I can break 72 into factors to make it easier to multiply. 72 = 8 × 9, so I can figure out 5 × 8 × 9.

$$5 \times 72$$
$$5 \times 8 \times 9$$

Step Up	**I.** Write an equation to show the order in which you would multiply these three numbers.

a.

| 5 | 7 | 2 |

5 × 2 × 7 = _____

b.

| 5 | 9 | 4 |

____ × ____ × ____ = _____

c.

| 5 | 7 | 6 |

____ × ____ × ____ = _____

d.

| 7 | 4 | 5 |

____ × ____ × ____ = _____

2. Break the number in the circle into two factors to make it easier to multiply. Write the matching equation.

a.

$5 \times \boxed{18} =$ _____

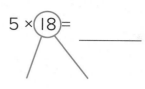

5 $\times$ 2 $\times$ ___ $=$ ___

b.

$5 \times \boxed{24} =$ _____

5 $\times$ 4 $\times$ ___ $=$ ___

c.

$25 \times \boxed{12} =$ _____

25 $\times$ ___ $\times$ ___ $=$ ___

d.

$5 \times \boxed{36} =$ _____

5 $\times$ ___ $\times$ ___ $=$ ___

3. Break **one number** into two factors to make it easier to multiply. Then complete the matching equation.

a.

$8 \times 45 =$ ⬚

___ $\times$ ___ $\times$ ___ $=$ ___

b.

$6 \times 35 =$ ⬚

___ $\times$ ___ $\times$ ___ $=$ ___

c.

$12 \times 15 =$ ⬚

___ $\times$ ___ $\times$ ___ $=$ ___

d.

$8 \times 55 =$ ⬚

___ $\times$ ___ $\times$ ___ $=$ ___

Step Ahead

This picture shows one crate of soda bottles.

Write an equation that shows the total number of bottles in five crates. Calculate the product in your head.

_____

Computation Practice

What is the offspring of a male horse and a female donkey called?

★ Complete the equations. Then find each product in the panel below and color the matching letter.

14 × 35 = ☐

18 × 25 = ☐

45 × 12 = ☐

12 × 15 = ☐

18 × 55 = ☐

35 × 16 = ☐

16 × 15 = ☐

45 × 18 = ☐

14 × 45 = ☐

12 × 55 = ☐

12 × 35 = ☐

15 × 14 = ☐

55 × 14 = ☐

45 × 16 = ☐

15 × 18 = ☐

16 × 55 = ☐

ORIGO *Stepping Stones* · Grade 4 · 11.6

© ORIGO Education

Ongoing Practice

1. Write the masses. Then write **<** or **>** to make a true statement.

	Patch	◯		Pepper

	Patch	◯		Snowy

What Our Cats Weigh	
Snowy	4.35 kg
Pepper	5.62 kg
Neddy	3.45 kg
Patch	4.53 kg
Jasper	4.26 kg

	Jasper	◯		Snowy

	Jasper	◯		Neddy

	Pepper	◯		Jasper

	Neddy	◯		Patch

2. Double one number and halve the other to make a problem that is easier to solve. Then write the product.

a. 35×14

_____ × _____

$35 \times 14 =$ ☐

b. 18×15

_____ × _____

$18 \times 15 =$ ☐

c. 45×8

_____ × _____

$45 \times 8 =$ ☐

d. 15×26

_____ × _____

$15 \times 26 =$ ☐

e. 35×24

_____ × _____

$35 \times 24 =$ ☐

f. 28×15

_____ × _____

$28 \times 15 =$ ☐

Preparing for Module 12

These clocks all show times after noon on the same day. Calculate the length of each trip.

a. Bus Departs   Bus Arrives

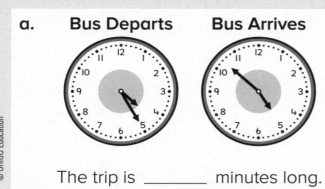

The trip is _____ minutes long.

b. Bus Departs   Bus Arrives

The trip is _____ minutes long.

Step In

There are 15 small boxes inside each of these large boxes.

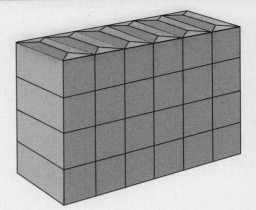

Write an equation you could use to calculate the total number of small boxes in all the large boxes.

How would you calculate the total in your head?

> I'd use factors to make the multiplication easier.

How would you multiply 3 × 5 × 6 × 4?
Which factors would you multiply first? Why?

What is the total number of small boxes?

15 × 6 × 4

is the same value as

3 × 5 × 6 × 4

Matthew counted 36 pine trees in one square of this field.

How could he estimate the total number of trees in the whole field if there are the same number in each square?

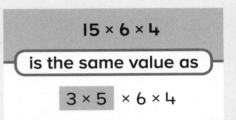

Step Up

1. Break **one** number into two factors to make it easier to multiply. Then complete the equation.

a.
35 × 8   is the same value as   ☐ × ☐ × ☐ = ☐

b.
6 × 35   is the same value as   ☐ × ☐ × ☐ = ☐

c.
25 × 28   is the same value as   ☐ × ☐ × ☐ = ☐

d.
45 × 4   is the same value as   ☐ × ☐ × ☐ = ☐

2. Break **both** numbers into two factors. Then write an equation showing the four factors in the order you would multiply them and calculate the product.

a.

40×18 **is the same value as**

☐ × ☐ × ☐ × ☐

☐ = ☐

b.

36×15 **is the same value as**

☐ × ☐ × ☐ × ☐

☐ = ☐

c.

12×30 **is the same value as**

☐ × ☐ × ☐ × ☐

☐ = ☐

d.

14×45 **is the same value as**

☐ × ☐ × ☐ × ☐

☐ = ☐

e.

25×16 **is the same value as**

☐ × ☐ × ☐ × ☐

☐ = ☐

Step Ahead

For each of these, write the product. Then write the different pairs of **two-digit** numbers that may have been factored to create these equations.

a.

$5 \times 2 \times 6 \times 9 = $ ☐

_____

_____

b.

$3 \times 5 \times 8 \times 7 = $ ☐

_____

_____

© ORIGO Education

Step In

What is the total cost of buying four tickets to Reptile Park? How do you know?

REPTILE PARK $35

What are some different strategies you could use to calculate the total cost?

I could halve one factor and double the other. That is 2 × 70.

Or I could break 35 into two factors and think 4 × 5 × 7.

What is another way you could calculate the total cost?

A store manager orders five boxes of pencils. Each box contains seven packs of pencils. Each pack holds eight pencils.

How could you calculate the total number of pencils ordered?

Which numbers would you multiply first?
Write an equation to show how you would multiply.

☐ × ☐ × ☐ = ☐

Step Up

1. Write an equation to represent each problem. Use a letter to represent the unknown amount. You do not need to calculate the final answer.

a. There are 2 boxes of apples. Each box holds 9 bags, and each bag holds 5 apples. How many apples in total?

b. A chessboard is made of 8 rows and 8 columns. How many small playing squares would you count on 5 chessboards?

© ORIGO Education

2. Solve each problem. Show your thinking.

a. There are 6 rows of 3 seats in each roller coaster car. There are 5 cars. What is the total number of seats?

_____ seats

b. A tent costs $39. Another tent costs 5 times as much. Three friends share the cost of the more expensive tent. How much does each person pay?

$_____

c. Patricia buys 8 shirts for $15 each. She uses a $25 gift card and cash to pay for the shirts. How much cash does she need to use?

$_____

d. There are 25 fish in each tank. There are 6 tanks. Another 2 fish are added to each tank. What is the total number of fish?

_____ fish

Step Ahead Write a word problem to match this equation. $15 \times A = 75$

Think and Solve

There is a total of 20 counters in the four boxes.
Use the clues to calculate how many are in each box.

Clues

- Box A has twice as many counters as Box B.

- Box C has 2 more counters than Box B.

- Box D has 2 fewer counters than Box B.

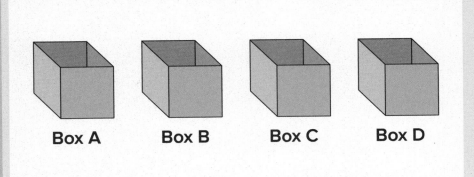

Box A   Box B   Box C   Box D

Box A has _____ counters   Box B has _____ counters

Box C has _____ counters   Box D has _____ counters

Words at Work   Write in words how you would solve this problem.

A factory produces 1,000 cans of beans each hour. The packing boxes hold 7 rows of 5 cans. How many full boxes of cans can be packed each hour?

Ongoing Practice

1. Write each total as a **common** fraction and **decimal** fraction.

a.
$$\frac{7}{10} + \frac{20}{100} = \frac{\boxed{}}{100} = \boxed{}$$

b.
$$\frac{2}{10} + \frac{45}{100} = \frac{\boxed{}}{100} = \boxed{}$$

c.
$$1\frac{6}{10} + \frac{12}{100} = \frac{\boxed{}}{100} = \boxed{}$$

d.
$$3\frac{22}{100} + \frac{5}{10} = \frac{\boxed{}}{100} = \boxed{}$$

2. Break **one** or **both** numbers into two factors to make it easier to multiply. Then write an equation showing the factors in the order you would multiply them to calculate the product.

a. 16×35

is the same value as

b. 14×55

is the same value as

c. 24×15

is the same value as

Preparing for Module 12

Color the bills and coins you would use to pay the **exact** price.

a. ○$2 and 35¢

b. ○$5 and 36¢

Step In   A straight line continues in both directions forever.

When you draw a straight line, it is just a part of a longer continuous line. This part is called a **line segment**.

> A **line segment** has a start point and an end point.

Look at the line below. The arrows show that it continues in both directions forever. Points A, B, and C are all on the same line.

All the points beginning at Point A and ending at Point B form one line segment, $\overline{AB}$. What other line segments are part of this line?

Point B splits the line into two parts. Each part is called a half line or a ray. A ray is named with its start point written first, followed by another point that the ray goes through.

> A **ray** is part of a line that begins at a point and continues on forever.

Look at the line above.
If Point B is the start point, the two rays $\overrightarrow{BC}$ and $\overrightarrow{BA}$ go in opposite directions.

Polygons can be described by naming the line segments that make their sides, or the points that are the vertices. This can help identify shapes.

Use a color pencil to trace over the polygon made by joining the points A, C, G, and F. What shape is it?

What other polygons can you see and describe?

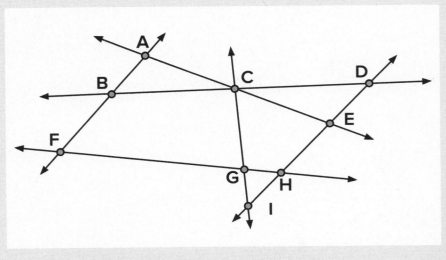

1. Name five unique line segments you can see on the line below.

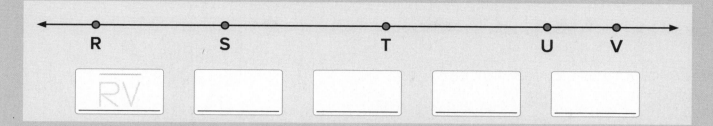

R   S   T   U   V

RV   [   ]   [   ]   [   ]   [   ]

2. Look at the line above. Name a pair of rays that start at each of these end points.

a. Point S	b. Point T	c. Point U
[ ] and [ ]	[ ] and [ ]	[ ] and [ ]

3. Look at the picture below.

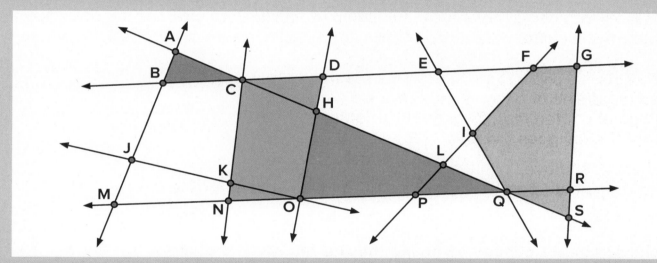

Write the points that make up the **vertices** of each shaded polygon.

Blue [_____]   Green [_____]   Red [_____]   Orange [_____]

Look at the picture in Question 3. Find other examples of each polygon below. Write the points that are the vertices of each shape.

a. triangle [_____]

b. quadrilateral [_____]

c. pentagon [_____]

d. hexagon [_____]

Step In   What do you know about parallel lines?

> When two lines are the same distance apart for their entire lengths, they are **parallel**.

Where might you see parallel lines?

Which two line segments below are parallel? How do you know?

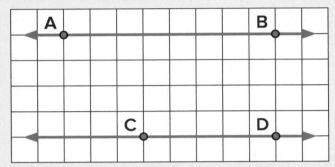
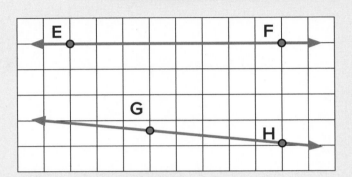

Parallel line segments do not have to be directly opposite each other, or the same length. If the lines that they are part of are parallel, then the line segments will also be parallel.

The line segment $\overline{JK}$ below is parallel to line segment $\overline{ST}$ and also to line segment $\overline{TU}$.

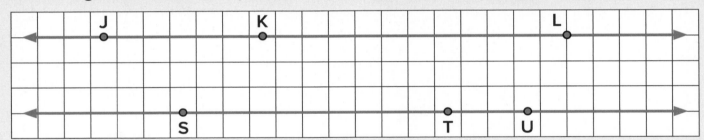

Which other line segments are parallel?

Perpendicular lines make a right angle with each other. The yellow line is perpendicular to the purple line.

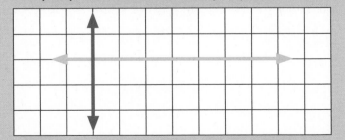

Perpendicular lines do not have to be vertical or horizontal. These lines are also perpendicular to each other.

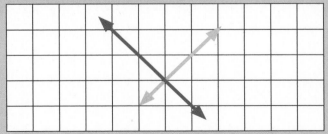

Perpendicular line segments do not need to intersect one another.

However, the lines that they are part of must intersect.

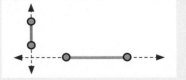

Step Up

Cut out the shapes from the support page and paste them in the correct spaces below. Some shapes do not belong in any of the spaces.

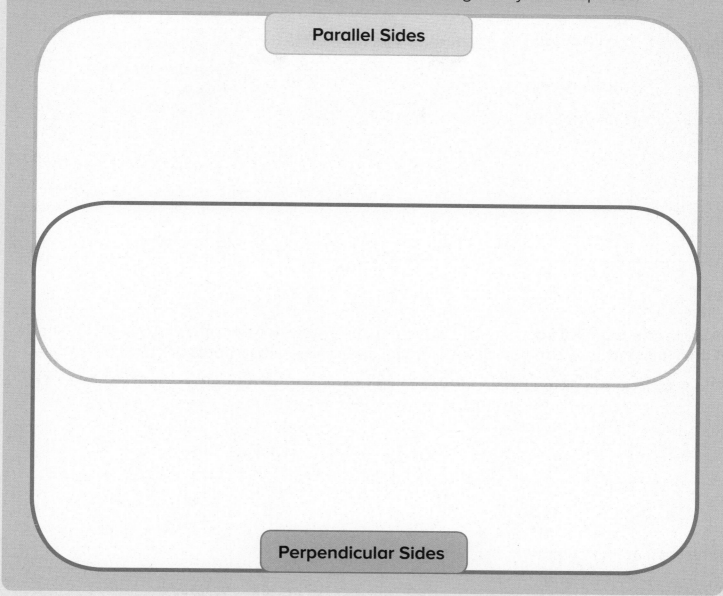

Parallel Sides

Perpendicular Sides

Step Ahead

Draw a square and a non-square rectangle. One side of each has been drawn for you. Use a protractor to check your drawings.

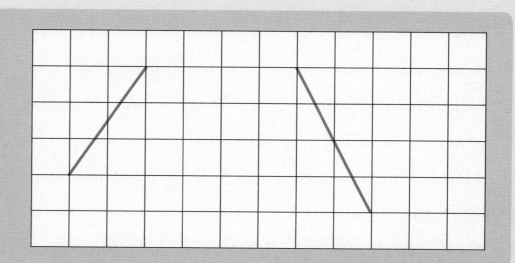

Computation Practice   What do you take off just before getting into bed?

★ Complete the equations. Then write each letter above its matching product at the bottom of the page.

$8 \times 4 \times 2 =$ _____ **o**

$5 \times 3 \times 7 =$ _____ **f**

$6 \times 2 \times 8 =$ _____ **e**

$4 \times 5 \times 6 =$ _____ **u**

$7 \times 2 \times 9 =$ _____ **e**

$2 \times 5 \times 8 =$ _____ **o**

$5 \times 6 \times 2 =$ _____ **f**

$9 \times 5 \times 3 =$ _____ **y**

$7 \times 5 \times 2 =$ _____ **h**

$4 \times 7 \times 3 =$ _____ **r**

$7 \times 6 \times 4 =$ _____ **r**

$4 \times 7 \times 5 =$ _____ **o**

$8 \times 9 \times 4 =$ _____ **t**

$7 \times 4 \times 8 =$ _____ **t**

$3 \times 6 \times 4 =$ _____ **o**

$9 \times 3 \times 4 =$ _____ **f**

$9 \times 3 \times 2 =$ _____ **f**

$8 \times 5 \times 4 =$ _____ **l**

$2 \times 0 \times 7 =$ _____ **e**

Working Space

135   72   120   168   54   0   126   224   140   105   60

288   70   96   108   160   80   64   84

ORIGO Stepping Stones · Grade 4 · 11.10

© ORIGO Education

Ongoing Practice

1. These are masses of different watermelons. Record each mass on the line plot below. You will need to convert the grams to kilograms.

7,500 g	5 $\frac{1}{2}$ kg	3 kg	6 kg	2 $\frac{1}{2}$ kg	5,500 g	5 kg	2,500 g	4,500 g
2 kg	5 $\frac{1}{2}$ kg	6 kg	4 $\frac{1}{2}$ kg	5 kg	5,500 g	6 $\frac{1}{2}$ kg	5 kg	3 $\frac{1}{2}$ kg

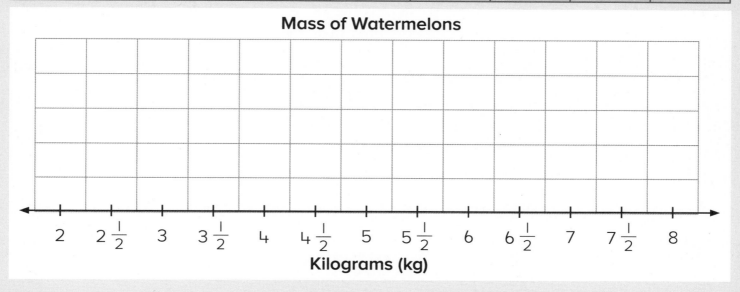

Mass of Watermelons

Kilograms (kg)

2. a. Name the unique line segments you can see on the line below.

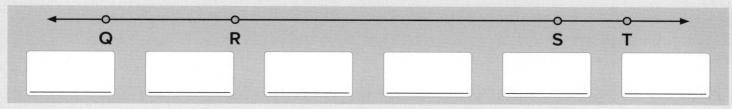

b. Name a pair of rays that start at each of these points.

Point R _____ and _____

Point S _____ and _____

Preparing for Module 12

Color the bills and coins you should use to pay the price. Then write the change you should receive.

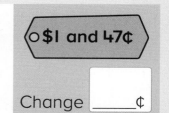

$1 and 47¢

Change _____ ¢

Step In Imagine you were wearing this shirt and looked in the mirror.

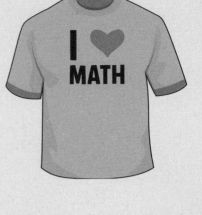

What would the shirt look like?

What words can you use to describe what mirrors do?

When I look in the mirror, I see my reflection.

Some shapes have parts that are a reflection of each other.
Draw the other half of the letter M on the other side of the dashed line. How will you know it is a reflection?

What other letters have two sides that are a reflection of each other?

Step Up I. Draw the reflection of each shape on the other side of the dashed line.

a.
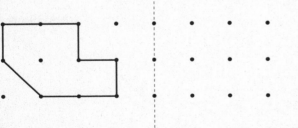

b.

c.
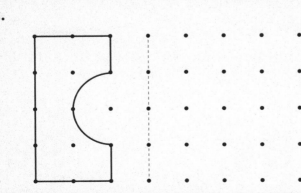

d.

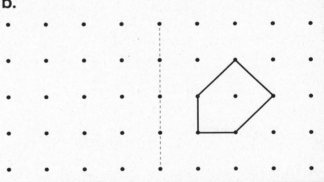

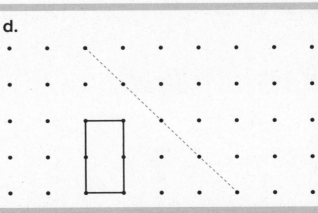

2. Draw the reflection on the other side of the dashed line.

a.
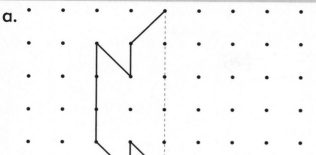

b.
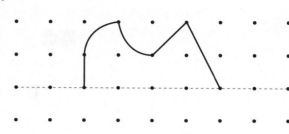

c.
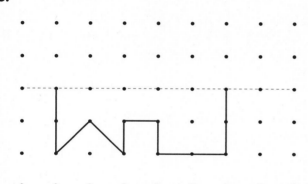

d.
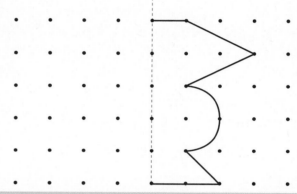

e.
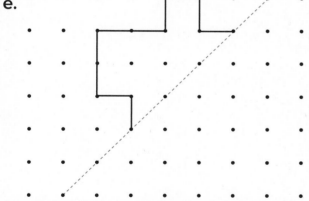

f.
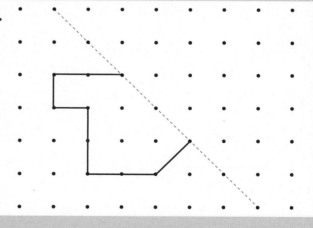

| **Step Ahead** | Draw on the left what the numbers 7, 35, and 86 would look like when reflected in a mirror. |

| 7 | 35 | 86 |

Step In

Draw a line of symmetry on each shape so one side of the shape is a mirror image of the other.

A **line of symmetry** splits a whole shape into two parts that are the same shape and the same size.

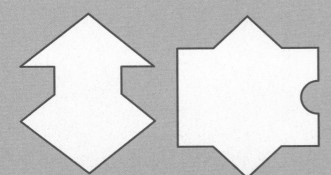

Try cutting and folding shapes like these to check your work.

How did you know where to draw the line on each shape?

Step Up

1. Find and draw the line of symmetry on each of these.

a.
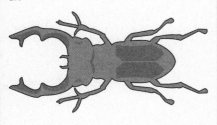

b.

c.

d.

e.

f.

© ORIGO Education

2. Find and draw the line of symmetry on each shape.

a.
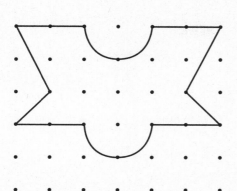

b.
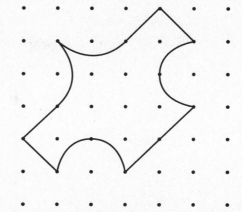

c.
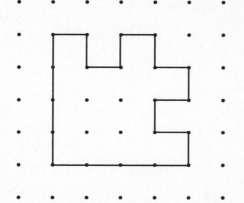

d.
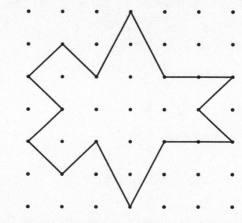

Step Ahead

Draw one shape that has a line of symmetry. Show the line of symmetry on the shape. Then draw one shape that has no lines of symmetry.

a.

b.

Think and Solve Look at this diagram.

Multiples of 2	2	Factors of 18

Write each of these numbers in the correct part of the diagram.

| 10 | 3 | 12 | 9 | 4 | 20 | 6 |

Words at Work Write words from the list to complete true sentences.

ray
symmetry
polygon
parallel
right
intersect
same
reflection
angle
segment
arrow
line

a. A line _____ has a start point and an end point.

b. A _____ is part of a line that begins at a point and continues on forever in one direction.

c. A _____ of _____ splits a whole shape into two parts that are the same shape and size.

d. _____ lines are the _____ distance apart for their entire lengths.

e. Perpendicular lines make a _____ _____ with each other.

Ongoing Practice

1. This line plot shows the lengths of some garden worms. Use this line plot to answer the questions below.

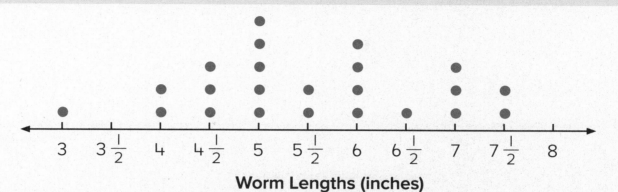

Worm Lengths (inches)

a. How many worms were measured? ⬚

b. Which length was recorded most frequently? ⬚ inches

c. What length is the shortest worm? ⬚ inches

d. How many worms were longer than 7 inches? ⬚

e. What is the difference in length between the longest and shortest worms? ⬚ inches

2. Write what you know about **parallel** lines. Then draw a pair of parallel lines on the grid.

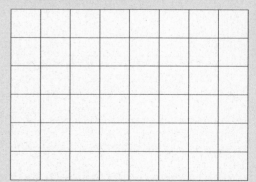

Preparing for Module 12

Think of a multiplication fact to help you solve each division problem. Then write the answers.

a. 16 ÷ 3 = ⬚ remainder ⬚

b. 37 ÷ 7 = ⬚ remainder ⬚

c. 46 ÷ 6 = ⬚ remainder ⬚

d. 67 ÷ 8 = ⬚ remainder ⬚

FROM 3.6.12

FROM 4.11.10

12.1 Patterns: Working with multiplication and addition patterns

Step In Books can be downloaded from a website for $3 each.

Ben has recorded the total cost for buying different numbers of books.

Number of Books	1	2	3	4	5
Total Cost ($)	3	6	9	12	

What is the total cost for buying five books? How did you figure it out?

Paige downloads apps that are $4 each.
Complete the table to show the total cost for downloading different numbers of apps.

Number of Apps	1	2	3	5	8
Total Cost ($)					

What would you do to calculate the cost of buying ten apps?

What rule could you use to calculate the cost of buying any number of apps?

What could you write to explain it?

To figure out the cost of any number of apps,
I could write: Number of apps × $4 = Total price.

Step Up 1. Complete the tables.

a. **Movies cost $8 each**

Number of Movies	Rule	Total Cost ($)
1	1 × 8	8
2	2 × 8	
5	5 × 8	
7	7 × 8	

b. **Movies cost $6 each**

Number of Movies	Rule	Total Cost ($)
1	1 × 6	
2		
5		
7		

2. A book store gives away 2 paperback books with every purchase. Complete the table to show the total number of books a customer would receive.

Books Bought	2	3	4	5		9
Rule	2 + 2	3 + 2	4 + 2	5 + 2		
Number of Books Received	4	5			9	

3. Read the rule. Then complete the table.

a. Number of pans × 4 = Number of mini-pizzas

Number of Pans	1	2		6		9
Number of Mini-Pizzas			16		28	

b. Number of tickets × 7 = Total price

Number of Tickets	1	3	5	8	9	10
Total Price ($)						

Step Ahead

Yuma hires a private room at a restaurant for a party. The food for each guest costs the same amount. The room costs $20 no matter how many people are there.

Look at the total costs she figured out.

Number of Guests	1	2	3	4
Total Price ($)	29	38	47	56

Write a rule to calculate the total cost for nine guests.

© ORIGO Education

Step In

Look at this growing pattern. How many squares are in the first picture? How many squares have been added to make the second picture?

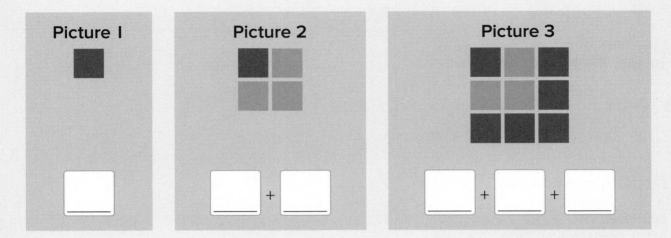

Picture 1	Picture 2	Picture 3

Picture 1: [ ]

Picture 2: [ ] + [ ]

Picture 3: [ ] + [ ] + [ ]

How many squares have been added to make the third picture?

What do you think the fourth and fifth pictures will look like?

Amy makes this table to help look for a pattern rule.

Picture Number	1	2	3	4	5	8	10
Number of Squares	1	4	9				

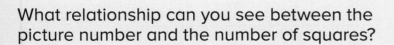

The picture number also tells the number of small squares along each side of the large square.

What relationship can you see between the picture number and the number of squares?

What rule could you use to calculate the number of squares for any picture number?

Complete the table.

> The product of a number multiplied by itself is called a **square number**. All square numbers can be represented as a square array.

© ORIGO Education

1. Use the square number rule to write the missing numbers. Show your calculations on page 470.

Picture Number	12	9	7	11			20
Number of Squares	144		49		36	225	

2. Complete each sentence. Show your thinking.

a. The square number closest to 300 is _____ .

b. The square number closest to 450 is _____ .

3. Norton is exploring square number patterns where there is a 2 in the ones place of the original number. His results are shown in this table.

Original number	12	22	32	42	52
Square number	144	484	1,024	1,764	2,704

a. Look at his pattern. Circle the numbers below that you think are square numbers.

| 6,241 | 5,184 | 2,401 | 6,724 | 9,409 | 8,649 |

b. Explain your thinking. _____

_____

_____

Find another square number pattern like the pattern in Question 3. Write what you find here.

_____

_____

Computation Practice

Which bird is so tiny that one of its enemies is the praying mantis?

★ Complete the equations. Then write each letter above its matching answer at the bottom of the page.

$(5 + 14) \times 8 =$ _____ **m** $4 \times (3 + 15) =$ _____ **b**

$5 \times (8 + 45) =$ _____ **h** $(75 + 6) \times 3 =$ _____ **n**

$(25 + 7) \times 4 =$ _____ **e** $5 \times (6 + 35) =$ _____ **i**

$3 \times (15 + 7) =$ _____ **t** $(25 + 9) \times 8 =$ _____ **i**

$(45 + 8) \times 4 =$ _____ **u** $6 \times (15 + 8) =$ _____ **r**

$8 \times (35 + 7) =$ _____ **h** $(45 + 8) \times 8 =$ _____ **d**

$(4 + 35) \times 6 =$ _____ **g** $4 \times (9 + 25) =$ _____ **m**

Working Space

66   265   128

336   212   136   152   272   243   234   72   205   138   424

Ongoing Practice

1. Write what you know about **perpendicular** lines.
    Then draw a pair of perpendicular lines on the grid.

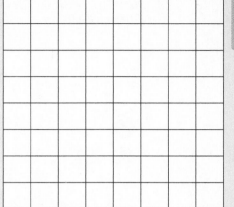

2. Read the rule. Then complete the table.

    a. Number of boxes × 9 = Number of bottles

Number of Boxes	1	2		5	10
Number of Bottles			27		

    b. Number of vases × 6 = Number of flowers

Number of Vases	1	2		7	
Number of Flowers			18		54

Preparing for Next Year

Draw extra beads on the abacus to match the number on the expander.

a.

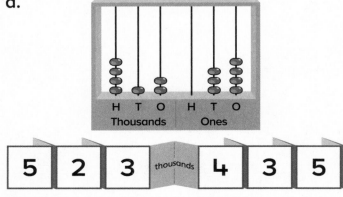

b.

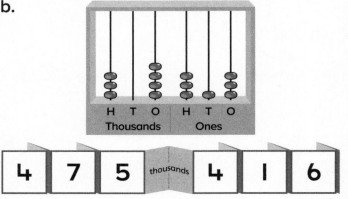

What can you tell about this growing pattern?

Picture 1	Picture 2	Picture 3

What do you think the fourth and fifth pictures will look like?

Peter makes this table to represent the pattern.

Picture Number	1	2	3	4	7	10	15
Number of Circles	3	5	7				

What relationship can you see between the
picture number and the number of circles?

> The number of circles is one more
> than double the picture number.

Do you think the 15th picture will have an odd or even number of circles?
How can you tell?

Complete the table.

Why is the number of circles always odd? Explain your thinking.

1. a. Read the rule. Then complete the table.

Number of circles = Picture number × 2

Picture Number	6	4	5	20	2	15	
Number of Circles		8		40	4		26

b. Do you think it is possible to record an odd number of circles? Explain your thinking.

2. a. Read the rule. Then complete the table.

Number of squares = Picture number + 3

Picture Number		5	1		20	7	15
Number of Squares	7		4	40	23		18

b. Do you think it is possible to record an odd picture number and an odd number of squares? Explain your thinking.

Look for a pattern rule. Then complete the table.

Picture Number	3	5	2	7		15	18
Number of Triangles	5	9	3		19		

Patterns: Analyzing shape patterns

Step In

Joel is decorating the school gymnasium.
He makes this repeating pattern.

What color flag should he hang next?
How can you tell?

How could you figure out the color of the 20th flag?

Joel creates this table.

How could it help him figure out
the color of the 20th flag?

What is the color of the 90th flag?
How do you know?

Red	White	Blue
1st	2nd	3rd
4th	5th	6th
7th	8th	9th

The position of each blue flag
is a multiple of 3.
90 is a multiple of 3, so the
90th flag will be blue.

Step Up

1. Continue each pattern.

a.

b.

c.

© ORIGO Education

2. a. Imagine this pattern continues. Draw the next shape in the pattern.

b. Draw the shape you would show in each of these positions.

20th   30th   45th   70th

Working Space

3. a. Imagine this pattern continues. Draw the next shape in the pattern.

b. Draw the shape you would show in each of these positions.

15th   50th   80th   99th

Working Space

Step Ahead   Solve this problem. Show your thinking on page 470.

Yasmin is making a bracelet. She threads one blue bead, two red beads, and then one yellow bead. She repeats this pattern until there are no beads left.

30 beads are used to make the bracelet.
What color is the last bead that she threads?

Think and Solve Read the clues. Write the matching number.

Clues

All of the digits are different.

The tenths digit is the greatest prime number less than 10.

The sum of the thousands and hundreds digits is equal to the tenths digit.

The hundreds digit is one more than the thousands digit.

The ones digit is a multiple of 5 and a prime number.

The tens digit is 4 less than the hundreds digit.

☐ ☐ ☐ ☐ . ☐

Words at Work   Research and write about where you see shape or number patterns in everyday life.

_____

_____

_____

_____

_____

_____

_____

_____

_____

Ongoing Practice

1. Name the shape. Then write what you know about the shape.

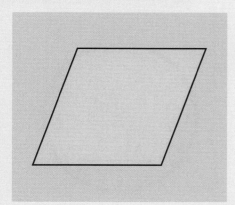

This shape is a _____

_____

_____

_____

FROM 4.11.10

2. Look at this pattern.

 Picture 1   △△ Picture 2   Picture 3   Picture 4

FROM 4.12.3

a. Draw the next two pictures in the pattern.

Picture 5

Picture 6

b. Complete this table to match.

Picture Number	1	2				
Number of Triangles	2					

Preparing for Next Year

Draw a line to connect each number to its position on the number line.

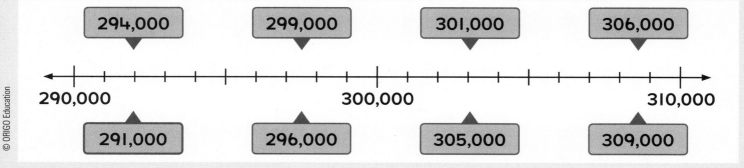

294,000   299,000   301,000   306,000

290,000   300,000   310,000

291,000   296,000   305,000   309,000

Step In Read the time on this clock.

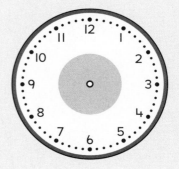

What do you do at about this time?

What other information do you need to know?

Draw hands on this clock to show the same time.

What are all the different ways you could say this time?
How can you figure out the number of minutes **to the hour**
when you know the number of minutes **past the hour?**

> I know the time is 45 minutes past the hour.
> I can figure out the number of minutes
> to the hour by thinking 45 + ? = 60.

Read the time on this clock.

9:37

How many minutes to 10 o'clock? How do you know?

Write an equation to show your thinking.

[   ]

Step Up   1. A train leaves Central Station at 3 o'clock. Look at each watch below.
             How many minutes does each person need to wait for the train?

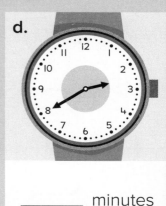

a. _____ minutes   b. _____ minutes   c. _____ minutes   d. _____ minutes

2. Write these times using **minutes to.**

a.
 _____ minutes

to _____

b.
 _____ minutes

to _____

c.
 _____ minutes

to _____

d.
 _____ minutes

to _____

3. Show the time on the analog and digital clocks.

a. 15 minutes to 3

b. 20 minutes to 5

c. 17 minutes to 6

d. 7 minutes to 9
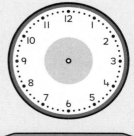

Step Ahead   Write the answers.

a. Arleen plays soccer at 4:30 on Wednesday afternoons. She plays for 45 minutes. What time does she finish?
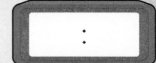

b. Steven catches a train at 7:55. The trip is expected to take 35 minutes. What time will he arrive?

c. Sharon leaves home at 6:45 and arrives at work at 7:32. How many minutes does it take her to travel to work?
_____ minutes

d. It takes Emilio 20 minutes to travel to school. If he gets to school at 8:18, at what time did he leave home?
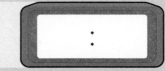

Step In

This table shows the length of time that activities took in one school day.

Activity	Time
Math	1 hour
Reading	55 minutes
Writing	30 minutes
Library	30 minutes
Science	30 minutes
Art	25 minutes
Sport	45 minutes
Music	25 minutes
Social Studies	30 minutes

What is the total length of time for math and science? How could you calculate the total in minutes?

1 hour + 30 minutes is equivalent to

_____ minutes

What are some other times in the table that total more than one hour?

Step Up

1. Write the total time. Then calculate the total in minutes.

a.
Rode to store	28 minutes
Shopped for DVDs	1 hour

_____ hour _____ minutes

_____ minutes

b.
Watched TV	2 hours
Read book	58 minutes

_____ hours _____ minutes

_____ minutes

c.
Ate breakfast	9 minutes
Swam in pool	3 hours
Ate lunch	35 minutes

_____ hours _____ minutes

_____ minutes

d.
Mowed lawn	1 hour
Trimmed hedges	12 minutes
Raked leaves	9 minutes

_____ hour _____ minutes

_____ minutes

2. Write the total time in two different ways.

a. In a triathlon, Sandra swam for 27 minutes, cycled for 35 minutes, and ran for 23 minutes. How long did it take her to finish the course?

_____ minutes

_____ hour _____ minutes

b. One show goes for 33 minutes. The next show is 15 minutes longer. What is the total time of the two shows?

_____ hour _____ minutes

_____ minutes

c. It takes 25 minutes to prepare dinner, and 3 times as long to cook it. What is the total time needed to prepare and cook the meal?

_____ minutes

_____ hour _____ minutes

d. Olivia has $2\frac{1}{4}$ hours to complete an exam. Part A takes 53 minutes, and Part B takes 25 minutes. How much time is left to complete Part C?

_____ hour _____ minutes

_____ minutes

Step Ahead   Calculate the total time for each trip.

a.

Fly San Jose to Los Angeles	40 min
Stopover in Los Angeles	35 min
Fly Los Angeles to Denver	1 hr 50 min

Total time

_____ hours _____ minutes

b.

Fly Houston to Atlanta	2 hr 10 min
Stopover in Atlanta	50 min
Fly Atlanta to Richmond	1 hr 40 min

Total time

_____ hours _____ minutes

Computation Practice

★ Complete the equations. Then write each letter above its matching product at the bottom of the page to find a fact about the natural world. Some letters are used more than once.

2 × 6 × 3 = _____ **e**   7 × 8 × 2 = _____ **l**   9 × 2 × 8 = _____ **a**

7 × 5 × 3 = _____ **o**   8 × 4 × 5 = _____ **i**   6 × 5 × 7 = _____ **s**

2 × 7 × 9 = _____ **t**   5 × 6 × 4 = _____ **r**   4 × 2 × 6 = _____ **u**

2 × 8 × 6 = _____ **y**   6 × 2 × 7 = _____ **m**   3 × 5 × 9 = _____ **d**

8 × 5 × 6 = _____ **o**   9 × 6 × 2 = _____ **q**   9 × 2 × 9 = _____ **c**

4 × 7 × 2 = _____ **s**   8 × 7 × 5 = _____ **t**   5 × 2 × 6 = _____ **f**

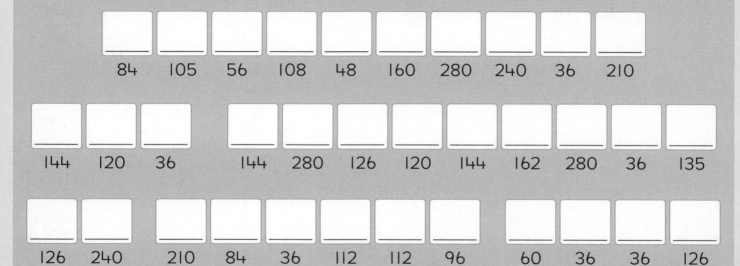

84   105   56   108   48   160   280   240   36   210

144   120   36   144   280   126   120   144   162   280   36   135

126   240   210   84   36   112   112   96   60   36   36   126

© ORIGO Education

Ongoing Practice

1. Find and draw the line of symmetry on each of these shapes.

a.
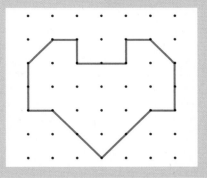

b.
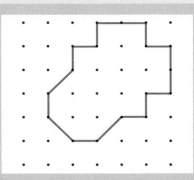

c.
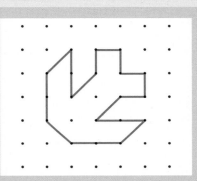

d.
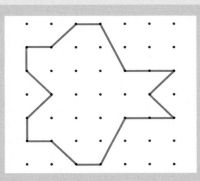

FROM 4.11.12

2. A train leaves North Station at 5 o'clock. Look at each watch below. How many minutes does each person need to wait for the train?

a.

_____ minutes

b.

_____ minutes

c.

_____ minutes

d.
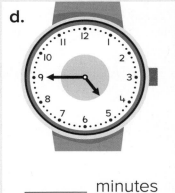
_____ minutes

FROM 4.12.5

Preparing for Next Year

Write **<** or **>** to make each statement true.

a. 223,715 ◯ 223,751

b. 116,059 ◯ 115,999

c. 375,210 ◯ 257,899

d. 410,502 ◯ 510,512

e. 753,650 ◯ 735,750

f. 119,007 ◯ 119,700

Step In

How could you complete this sentence?

I am ____ years and ____ days old.

How can you figure out the exact number of days since you were born?
What do you need to know?

How many leap years have there been since you were born?
Use a calculator to figure out your age in days.

____ days

If it is 8:00 a.m., how could you figure out the time
that is 10 hours before?

I subtract 12 hours first, which
makes 8 p.m. Then I add on 2 hours.

What is another way you could do it?

How can you estimate the number of hours you could be at school in one year?

How many minutes could you be at school in one day?

Estimate the number of hours you sleep in one night. How many minutes is that?

Step Up

1. Write the current time on this clock.
   Use this time to answer Questions 2 to 5.

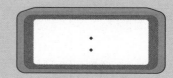

2. What time will it be after these minutes have passed?

a. 10 minutes

b. 90 minutes

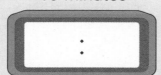

c. 600 minutes

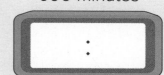

3. Complete these.

a. 10 minutes ago it was

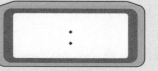

b. 90 minutes ago it was

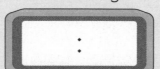

c. 600 minutes ago it was

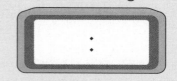

4. **a.** How many hours and minutes have passed since midnight last night?

_____

 b. Write your answer again in minutes. _____

5. **a.** How many hours and minutes will pass before midnight tonight?

_____

 b. Write your answer again in minutes. _____

6. Write the missing times.

a.

10 hours before				
Time	10:35 a.m.	11:09 p.m.	11:40 a.m.	7:20 p.m.
10 hours after				

b.

30 minutes before				
Time	10:35 a.m.	11:09 p.m.	11:40 a.m.	7:20 p.m.
30 minutes after				

c.

$2\frac{1}{2}$ hours before				
Time	10:35 a.m.	11:09 p.m.	11:40 a.m.	7:20 p.m.
$2\frac{1}{2}$ hours after				

Step Ahead   Write three times during the school day that are:

a.

75 minutes apart

⬚ : ⬚ → ⬚ : ⬚ → ⬚ : ⬚

b.

100 minutes apart

⬚ : ⬚ → ⬚ : ⬚ → ⬚ : ⬚

Step In   What do you notice about this clock?

What does the thin red hand represent?

Where have you seen or heard the word **seconds** used before?

What numbers will you say as the second hand moves around the clock?

What happens to the minute hand when the second hand passes 12?

How would you read the time on this clock? Do you say the number of seconds?

> The abbreviation for minute is min. The abbreviation for hour is h.

> Most people just want to know the number of minutes that have passed the hour, or the number of minutes to the next hour.

> There are 60 seconds in one minute. A short way to write second is s.

How could you calculate the total number of seconds in three minutes?

How could you calculate the total number of seconds in one and a half minutes?

Step Up   1. Complete each table.

a.

Minutes	Seconds
$\frac{1}{2}$	
1	60
5	
100	

b.

Hours	Minutes	Seconds
$\frac{1}{4}$		
$\frac{1}{2}$		
1	60	3,600
10		

© ORIGO Education

2. Solve each problem. Show your thinking.

a. The microwave instructions say to heat the pie on high for $4\frac{1}{2}$ minutes. Vincent stops the microwave after 3 minutes and 52 seconds. How many seconds are left on the microwave clock?

_____ s

b. Carmela has 2 minutes for a costume change. She takes 55 seconds to change clothes and 46 seconds to change shoes. How many seconds are left before she goes back on stage?

_____ s

c. At the start of the year, it took Michael $2\frac{1}{2}$ minutes to write the nines multiplication facts. It now takes him one minute and 39 seconds. By how many seconds has he improved?

_____ s

d. Zoe finished the race in one minute and 5 seconds. Her time was 11 seconds slower than the person who came second, and 26 seconds slower than the winner. What was the winner's race time?

_____ s

Step Ahead

Oliver used **one** cup of sand to make this timer. The timer goes for 20 seconds. It needs to run for exactly one minute so he decides to add more sand.

How many more cups of sand should he add?

_____ cups

Think and Solve

A, B, and C are different whole numbers.

What is the least number that C could be? ☐

$$A < B$$
$$B < C$$
$$A + B + C > 20$$

Words at Work

Write a word problem that requires you to add seconds. Then write how you find the solution.

_____

_____

_____

_____

_____

_____

_____

_____

_____

_____

_____

_____

_____

Ongoing Practice

1. Calculate the products. Show your thinking.

a.
25 × 18 = _____

b.
45 × 14 = _____

c.
28 × 35 = _____

d.
35 × 16 = _____

e.
25 × 14 = _____

f.
18 × 45 = _____

2. Complete each table.

a.

Minutes	Seconds
$\frac{1}{4}$	
1	60
4	
10	

b.

Hours	Minutes	Seconds
$\frac{1}{3}$	20	
$\frac{1}{2}$	30	
1	60	3,600
12		

Preparing for Next Year

Round each number to the nearest ten, hundred, and thousand.

	Nearest Ten	Nearest Hundred	Nearest Thousand
307,512			
628,168			
576,107			

Step In

What fraction of one dollar is one cent?

How would you write that as a decimal fraction?

What fraction of one dollar is twenty-five cents?

How would you write that as a decimal fraction?

What does a price like $3.16 mean?

Claire has this bill and coin in her purse, and she wants to buy the drink.

$1.85

How much more money does she need?
Claire counted on in her head like this.

 = $1.85

What is another way you could count on to $1.85?

Step Up

1. Draw the extra bills or coins you need to pay the **exact** price.

a.

 $1.60

b.

 $1.75

c.

 $3.10

2. Draw tallies to show the extra bills or coins you need to pay the **exact** price.

	ONE DOLLAR	QUARTER DOLLAR	ONE DIME	FIVE CENTS	ONE CENT
a. $2.95	||		||		
b. $2.41				||	
c. $3.50									
d. $5.16								
e. $4.11								
f. $3.10		||			

(Row d: | in ONE DOLLAR, | in FIVE CENTS; Row e: || in ONE DOLLAR, | in ONE CENT)

Step Ahead

Three friends want to buy a bag of water balloons for $4.95. Amos has 5 quarters, Emilia has 2 dollar bills, and Hassun has one dollar bill and 2 dimes. How much more money do they need? Show your thinking.

_____ ¢

GRANOLA BAR 70¢

Step In   Dallas pays for the granola bar with a $1 bill.

How much change should she be given? How do you know?

Dallas counts on to calculate the change. This diagram shows her strategy.

70¢ + 25¢ + 5¢ = $1

price   change   amount paid

What other coins could be given as change?

How could you use the change for $1 to quickly calculate the change for $5?

$2.15

If you use a $5 bill to buy this muffin, how much change will you receive? How do you know?

How much change will you receive if you buy two muffins?

Step Up   1.   Draw the coins you would receive as change.

Price	Amount you pay	Change you receive
a. 65¢	THE UNITED STATES OF AMERICA ONE DOLLAR	
b. TOMATOES $1.15	THE UNITED STATES OF AMERICA ONE DOLLAR QUARTER DOLLAR	
c. CHIPS $1.75	THE UNITED STATES OF AMERICA ONE DOLLAR THE UNITED STATES OF AMERICA ONE DOLLAR	

© ORIGO Education

2. Draw the bills or coins you would receive as change.

Price	Amount you pay	Change you receive
a. YOGHURT ○$2.25		
b. SNACK & DIP Six Pack ○$3.40	THE UNITED STATES OF AMERICA FIVE DOLLARS (\$5 bill)	
c. ice cream ○$4.75	THE UNITED STATES OF AMERICA TEN DOLLARS (\$10 bill)	

3. Write the amount you would receive as change.
You can draw bills or coins to help your thinking.

a. Paid $5 ○$3.98

Change _____

b. Paid $10 ○$6.35

Change _____

Step Ahead Imagine you bought the three items in Question 2 using a $20 bill. Estimate the total amount you would pay, and the change you would receive. Then use a calculator to check your estimates.

Amount you will pay

Estimate _____

Change you will receive

Estimate _____

Computation Practice

What is the difference between an Indian elephant and an African elephant?

★ Complete the equations. Then write each letter above its matching total at the bottom of the page. Some letters appear more than once.

$3.45 + $8.35 = $_____ **i** $2.55 + $3.15 = $_____ **h**

$6.35 + $5.25 = $_____ **a** $6.50 + $4.35 = $_____ **d**

$4.35 + $8.25 = $_____ **m** $6.65 + $8.15 = $_____ **s**

$7.55 + $4.15 = $_____ **r** $4.05 + $3.85 = $_____ **u**

$5.15 + $5.60 = $_____ **l** $8.20 + $7.05 = $_____ **b**

$5.55 + $1.05 = $_____ **e** $4.25 + $9.65 = $_____ **x**

$4.45 + $3.35 = $_____ **n** $9.40 + $6.15 = $_____ **k**

$8.30 + $3.55 = $_____ **o** $3.15 + $5.65 = $_____ **t**

$11.60	$15.25	$11.85	$7.90	$8.80		$14.80	$11.80	$13.90

$8.80	$5.70	$11.85	$7.90	$14.80	$11.60	$7.80	$10.85

$15.55	$11.80	$10.75	$11.85	$12.60	$6.60	$8.80	$6.60	$11.70	$14.80

Ongoing Practice

I. Break one number into two factors that are easier to multiply. Then write the matching equation.

a.

$6 \times 25 =$ _____

___ × ___ × ___ = _____

b.

$15 \times 8 =$ _____

___ × ___ × ___ = _____

c.

$45 \times 4 =$ _____

___ × ___ × ___ = _____

d.

$35 \times 8 =$ _____

___ × ___ × ___ = _____

2. Draw the bills and coins you would receive as change.

Price	Amount you pay	Change you receive
 PAPER $3.75		
CATS $4.45		

Preparing for Next Year

Calculate the part in the parentheses and write the new problem. Then write the answer.

a. $25 + (6 \times 5)$

= _____ + _____

= _____

b. $(30 + 6) \div 4$

= _____ ÷ _____

= _____

c. $(7 - 4) \times 8$

= _____ × _____

= _____

d. $30 - (30 \div 10)$

= _____ − _____

= _____

e. $18 + (16 \div 2)$

= _____ + _____

= _____

f. $200 + (3 \times 7)$

= _____ + _____

= _____

Step In

Four friends share the cost of this gift.
How much did each person pay?

$46

I know it is more than $10 each, because
4 × 10 is 40 and that is not enough.

Tyler uses play money to help calculate
the amount that each person should pay.

After sharing the amount he notices that
there are two $1 bills left over.

How can $2 be shared equally among 4?

What is the total amount that
each person should pay?

$2 has the same value as 200 cents.
I can share 200 equally among 4.

Step Up   1. Complete each of these.

a.
$1 shared between 2 is _____ cents each or $_____

b.
$1 shared between 4 is _____ cents each or $_____

c.
$1 shared between 5 is _____ cents each or $_____

d.
$1 shared between 10 is _____ cents each or $_____

2. Solve each problem. Show your thinking.

a. It costs $89 to stay at a campsite for two nights. What is the cost for one night?

$_____

b. It costs $50 to fill the truck with fuel. Four friends share the cost. How much should they each pay?

$_____

c. Four friends share the cost of a lunch. The meal costs $25. How much should they each pay?

$_____

d. It costs $56 to buy five movie tickets. What is the cost of one ticket?

$_____

Step Ahead   Solve this problem. There is more than one possible answer.

Daniel goes to dinner with some friends. They decide to share the total cost of the bill. Each person contributes the bills and coins shown in the picture.

a. What amount did each person pay? _____

b. What is the total cost of the meal? _____

c. How many people went to dinner? _____

Money: Solving word problems

Step In

Beatrice has six coins in her purse.
The total value of the coins is $0.86.

What coins are in her purse?
Draw pictures of coins to show your thinking.

> I started with quarters.
> 3 × 25¢ makes 75¢. That leaves
> only 3 coins to make 11 cents.

Gabriel has four coins and one bill in his wallet.
The total value of the bill and coins is $5.08.

What bill and coins are in his wallet?

What equation could you write to show your thinking?

How much more money does Gabriel have than Beatrice?
How would you calculate the difference?

Step Up

1. Solve each problem. Show your thinking.

a. Ashley has 3 $1 bills and one nickel in her money box. She finds 5
more quarters under the sofa. How much money does she now have?

$ _____

b. Tama has 3 quarters more than the total amount Eva has.
Tama has $1.25. How much does Eva have?

$ _____

2. Solve each problem. Show your thinking.

a. Grace has a $5 bill and 4 dimes. She spends some money at the store. She has 3 dollar bills and 2 quarters left. How much money did she spend?

$_____

b. Movies cost $7.45 to buy. Aston has one $5 bill, one $1 bill and 2 nickels. How much more money does he need to buy one movie?

$_____

c. Three friends compare the amount of money they have saved. Camila has $3.95, and Owen has $5.20. Fiona has saved $1.50 more than Camila. How much money has Fiona saved?

$_____

d. Allan takes his pocket money to the fun fair. He spends $4.50 on rides. He has one $1 bill, 2 dimes, and 3 pennies left in his wallet. How much money did he take to the fun fair?

$_____

Step Ahead

Cathy has $5.10 and Hugo has $7.20. They decide to share the cost of this gift. How much money would each person have left if they buy the gift?

$9

Cathy $_____

Hugo $_____

Think and Solve Use the clues to match each person to their shape.

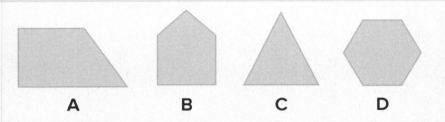

A   B   C   D

a. Mateo's shape is _____

b. Emily's shape is _____

c. Kayla's shape is _____

d. Cary's shape is _____

Clues

- Mateo's shape has 3 pairs of parallel sides.
- Emily's shape has 3 acute angles.
- Kayla's shape has 2 obtuse angles.
- Cary's shape does not have a line of symmetry.

Words at Work

Write in words how you solve this problem. There is more than one possible solution.

Kylie and Ethan have each saved some money. In their savings, each coin is worth less than 50 cents and each bill is less than $10. Kylie has saved more money than Ethan, but he has more bills and coins than Kylie. She has one bill and seven coins. What is the greatest amount of money each person could have?

© ORIGO Education

Ongoing Practice

1. Break **one** or **both** numbers into two factors to make it easier to multiply. Then write an equation showing the factors in the order you would multiply them to calculate the product.

a.
28 × 25   **is the same value as**
_____

b.
45 × 12   **is the same value as**
_____

c.
55 × 16   **is the same value as**
_____

d.
34 × 15   **is the same value as**
_____

2. Solve each problem. Show your thinking.

a. Jennifer has a $10 bill and 4 nickels. She spends some of the money at the store. She now has a $5 bill and 1 quarter and 1 nickel. How much money did she spend?

$ _____

b. DVDs are on sale for $6.15 each. Harvey has four $1 bills, 2 quarters, and 2 dimes. How much more money does he need to buy one movie?

$ _____

Preparing for Next Year

Write an equation to match each problem. Then write the answer.

a. Juan has $20. He buys lunch for $12, then shares the change equally between his two children. How much did they each receive?

$ _____

b. Jacinta has $50. She buys 3 tickets for $8 each. How much money does she have left?

$ _____

© ORIGO Education

STUDENT GLOSSARY

Algorithm

Algorithms are rules used for completing tasks or for solving problems. There are standard algorithms for calculating answers to addition, subtraction, multiplication and division problems. This example shows the division algorithm.

```
        2   0   8
  4 ) 8   3   2
    - 8   ↓   ↓
      0   3   2
        - 3   2
              0
```

Angle

An **acute angle** is an angle that is less than 90 degrees (90°). An **obtuse angle** is an angle that is greater than 90 degrees (90°) but less than 180 degrees (180°). A **right angle** is an angle that is equal to 90 degrees (90°).

Area

Area is the amount of surface that a shape covers. This amount is usually described in square units, such as square centimeters (cm²), or square inches (in²).

Capacity

Customary Units of Capacity		Metric Units of Capacity	
8 fluid ounces (fl oz)	I cup (c)	1,000 milliliters (mL)	I liter
2 cups	I pint (pt)		
2 pints	I quart (qt)		
4 quarts	I gallon (gal)		

Common fraction

$\frac{2}{3}$ is shaded

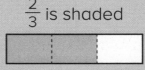

Common fractions describe equal parts of a whole. In this common fraction, 2 is the numerator and 3 is the denominator. The denominator shows the total number of equal parts (3). The numerator shows the number of those parts (2).

A **common denominator** is one that two or more fractions have in common.

Unit fractions are common fractions that have a numerator of 1.

Proper fractions are common fractions that have a numerator that is less than the denominator. For example, $\frac{2}{5}$ is a proper fraction.

Improper fractions are common fractions that have a numerator that is greater than or equal to the denominator. For example, $\frac{7}{5}$ and $\frac{4}{4}$ are improper fractions.

Equivalent fractions are fractions that cover the same amount of area on a shape or are located on the same point on a number line.

For example: $\frac{1}{2}$ is equivalent to $\frac{2}{4}$.

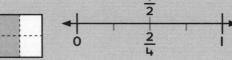

Comparing

When read from left to right, the symbol > means **is greater than**.
The symbol < means **is less than**. For example: 2 < 6 **means** 2 is less than 6

Composite number

A **composite number** is a whole number that has more than two whole number factors.

Decimal fraction

Decimal fractions are fractions in which the denominator is 10, 100, or 1,000, etc. but are always written using decimal points. For example: $\frac{3}{10}$ can be written as 0.3 and $\frac{28}{100}$ can be written as 0.28.

A **decimal point** indicates which digit is in the ones place. It is positioned immediately to the right of the ones digit. E.g. in the numeral 23.85, 3 is in the ones place.

A digit's **decimal place** is its position on the right-hand side of the decimal point. The first decimal place to the right of the decimal point is the tenths place. The next place is called hundredths. For example, in the numeral 23.85, 8 is in the first decimal place so it has the value of 8 tenths.

Degree

A **degree** is one unit of angle measure. There are 360 degrees in a full turn around a point. The symbol used to show degrees is °.

Expanded form

A method of writing numbers as the sum of the values of each digit.
E.g. 4,912 = (4 × 1,000) + (9 × 100) + (1 × 10) + (2 × 1)

Factor

Factors are whole numbers that evenly divide another whole number.
E.g. 4 and 5 are both factors of 20 and 20 is a multiple of both 4 and 5.

Length

Customary Units of Length		Metric Units of Length	
12 inches (in)	1 foot (ft)	10 millimeters (mm)	1 centimeter (cm)
3 feet	1 yard (yd)	100 centimeters	1 meter (m)
1,760 yards	1 mile (mi)	1,000 meters	1 kilometer (km)

STUDENT GLOSSARY

Line

A straight **line** continues in both directions forever. It never ends.

A **line segment** has a start point and an end point. It is part of a straight line that continues in both directions forever.

A **ray** is part of a line that begins at a point and continues on forever.

Line of symmetry

A **line of symmetry** splits a whole shape into two parts that are the same shape and the same size.

Mass (weight)

Customary Units of Mass		Metric Units of Mass	
16 ounces (oz)	I pound (lb)	1,000 grams (g)	I kilogram (kg)

Mixed number

A **mixed number** is a whole number and a common fraction added together, and written without the addition symbol. E.g.:

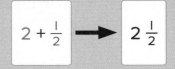

Multiple

Multiples of a number can be found by multiplying that number by other whole numbers. For example, the multiples of 4 include 4, 8, 12, and 16.

Parallel lines

Parallel lines are straight lines that are the same distance apart along their entire length.

Perimeter

A **perimeter** is the boundary of a shape and the total length of that boundary. For example, the perimeter of this rectangle is 20 inches.

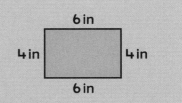

Perpendicular lines

Perpendicular lines are straight lines that make a right angle with each other.

STUDENT GLOSSARY

Prime number

A **prime number** is any whole number greater than zero that has exactly two unique factors — itself and 1.

Square number

A **square number** is one that can be shown as a square when arranged with dots. For example 1, 4, and 9 are the first three square numbers.

Time

| 60 seconds (s) | 1 minute (min) | 60 minutes | 1 hour (hr) |

Stem-and-leaf plot

A graph where data is organized by separating place values with a vertical line. For example, 13, 18, and 23 are shown as below.

Stem	Leaf	
1	3	8
2	3	

TEACHER INDEX

TEACHER INDEX

Division (continued)

Think multiplication 48, 110, 166, 167, 186, 212, 250, 251, 261

Related to multiplication 48, 110, 212, 249, 261, 282, 283

Remainders 250–3, 261, 292, 431, 464, 465

Three-digit numbers 64, 65, 67, 201, 290, 291, 294, 295, 299, 374

Two-digit numbers 11, 29, 137, 246, 247, 249, 255, 284, 285, 287–9, 293, 336, 431

Word problems 143, 164–7, 171, 213, 252, 253, 295, 301–3

Estimating

Addition 11, 17, 23, 44–7, 49–51, 53, 54, 56–9, 61, 62, 66, 87, 93, 99, 261

Angles 228, 229

Division 17

Multiplication 397, 399, 401–3, 407

Subtraction 87, 93, 99, 105, 111, 120, 121, 123, 125, 127, 128, 130, 131, 133–5, 299, 305

Fact family

Multiplication and division 249

Fractions

Common fractions

Addition 225, 256, 257, 262, 263, 267, 273, 348, 349, 385, 389, 419

Comparing 153, 266, 287, 293, 320–3, 325–7, 330–3, 337–43

Concepts 140

Equivalent 117, 144, 145, 149, 152, 153, 231, 299, 328, 329

Finding common denominators 334, 335, 338, 339, 342, 343

Improper fractions 144–7, 149–53, 219, 225, 231, 279

Language 150, 151

Mixed numbers 150–3, 155, 258, 259, 262, 263, 268–71, 273–5, 312–5, 317, 325, 331, 349, 366, 367, 369–71, 385, 389

Models

Area 111, 117, 140, 141, 143, 150–2, 155, 256, 267, 306, 307, 312–5, 325, 328, 393

Length 144, 145, 151, 155, 293, 322, 323

Number line 140, 141, 144, 145, 147, 149, 152, 153, 219, 256–9, 262, 264, 265, 268–71, 273, 287, 299, 311, 320, 321, 325–7, 331, 337

Fractions (continued)

Multiplication 306–9, 311–5, 317

Ordering 327, 341

Subtraction 264, 265, 268–71, 278, 279, 348

Unit fractions 267, 273, 393

Word problems 274, 275, 278, 307, 315

Decimal fractions

Addition 382–9, 392, 393, 462

Comparing 361, 378, 379, 413

Concepts 358, 360, 368

Hundredths 364–7, 369–71, 376, 377, 381, 384, 385, 388, 389, 393, 407, 413, 462

Models

Area 358, 359, 364–7, 369, 370, 388, 407

Number line 360, 361, 376–9, 381, 401

Ordering 379

Tenths 358–61, 363, 377, 381–3, 386–9, 401

Word problems 390, 391

Measurement

Area

Composite shapes 79, 343

Irregular polygons 206

Regular shapes 67, 73, 106, 107, 111, 114, 115, 175, 181, 196–9, 204, 231, 282, 283, 337

Rule for calculating 67, 106, 107

Word problems 79, 114, 115, 206

Capacity

Comparing 317

Conversion

Liters, milliliters 188, 189, 193, 201

Gallons, quarts, pints, cups, fluid ounces 350, 351, 354

Customary 317, 350, 351, 354

Language 350

Metric 143, 188–91, 201, 230, 368

Word problems 155, 190, 191, 207, 230, 351–3, 355

Length

Conversion

Feet, inches 210, 211

Kilometers, meters 182, 183, 187

Meters, centimeters 172, 173, 175, 187

Miles, yards, feet 216–8, 331

Millimeters, centimeters, meters 176–81

Yards, feet, inches 214, 215, 219, 325

Customary 175, 181, 210, 211, 214–9, 225

Data 210, 211, 276, 277

Language 176, 182

TEACHER INDEX

Measurement (continued)

Metric 137, 172, 173, 175–81, 187, 190, 191
Word problems 78, 175, 190, 191, 215

Mass
  Comparing 311, 345
  Conversion
    Kilograms, grams 184, 185, 190, 191, 363
    Pounds, ounces 346, 347, 349, 369
  Customary 311, 344–7, 349, 352, 353, 369
  Language 344
  Metric 116, 149, 184, 185, 190, 191
  Word problems 155, 190, 191, 278, 345, 347, 352, 353, 355

Perimeter
  Irregular polygons 35, 41
  Regular polygons 73, 108, 109, 112–5, 117, 187, 349, 355
  Rule for calculating 108, 109, 112, 113, 187
  Word problems 79, 114, 115, 180

Time
  Conversion
    Hours, minutes 448, 449
    Hours, minutes, seconds 454, 457
    Minutes, seconds 454, 455, 457
  Duration 104, 155, 413, 451
  Elapsed 452, 453, 456
  Minutes 149, 155, 273, 279, 407, 446, 447
  Seconds 454–6
  Word problems 104, 446, 447

Money

Cents 61
Dollars 61
Transactions 61, 67, 419, 425, 458–61, 463
Word problems 464–9

Multiplication

Basic facts
  All facts 22, 110, 186, 212, 261, 282, 283
  Eights 30, 31, 249
  Fives 35, 68, 69, 249
  Fours 30, 31
  Nines 48, 74, 75
  Sixes 48
  Tens 36, 37, 74, 75
  Threes 48
Estimating 397, 399, 401–3, 407
Factors 96, 97, 99–101, 104, 105, 305, 381
Four-digit numbers 202, 203, 207

Multiplication (continued)

Fractions
  Common fractions 306–9, 311, 316
  Mixed numbers 312–5, 317
Language 102, 103, 158, 159
Mental strategies
  Double and halve 61, 100, 101, 136, 375, 408, 409, 412, 413, 457
  Doubling (and repeated doubling) 30–3, 35, 86
  Partial products 163, 196–9, 201–5, 207, 213, 224, 255, 272, 279, 312, 313, 363, 396, 398, 402, 406
  Use a known fact 68–71, 73–9, 406
  Use factors 410, 411, 414, 415, 419, 463, 469
Models
  Array 28, 36, 37, 408
  Comparison 158–61, 163–5, 170, 171, 218
Multiples 96, 97, 99, 104, 292, 305, 309, 334, 335, 338
Patterns 38–41, 434–7, 439–41
Prime and composite numbers 102–4
Properties
  Associative 100, 101, 136, 408–15, 419, 424, 450, 457, 463, 469
  Commutative (turnaround) 31, 33, 37, 68, 69, 74, 75
  Distributive (partial products) 163, 196–9, 201–5, 207, 213, 224, 255, 272, 279, 312, 313, 363, 396, 398, 402, 406
Square numbers 436, 437
Standard algorithm 396, 397–9, 401–4, 407
Three-digit numbers 198, 199, 324
Two-digit numbers 26–8, 32, 33, 36, 37, 70, 71, 73, 76–9, 86, 124, 174, 196, 197, 201, 204, 205, 362, 363, 375, 396–9, 401–3, 407–15, 419, 457, 463, 469
Word problems 69, 159–61, 163–5, 168–71, 208, 209, 315, 369, 404, 405, 416, 417

Number line

Position 20, 21, 23, 55, 82, 88, 140, 141, 144, 145, 147, 149, 152, 153, 219, 287, 299, 320, 321, 325–7, 331, 337, 376–9, 401, 445
Recording mental strategies 11, 155, 256–9, 262, 264, 265, 268–71, 273, 279, 308, 311, 349